DAILY LIFE OF

WOMEN IN ANCIENT EGYPT

Recent Titles in
The Greenwood Press Daily Life Through History Series

DAILY LIFE OF

WOMEN IN ANCIENT EGYPT

LISA K. SABBAHY

The Greenwood Press Daily Life Through History Series

 GREENWOOD

An Imprint of ABC-CLIO, LLC

Santa Barbara, California • Denver, Colorado

Library of Congress Cataloging-in-Publication Data

Names: Sabbahy, Lisa, author.
Title: Daily life of women in ancient Egypt / Lisa K. Sabbahy.
Description: Santa Barbara, California : Greenwood, [2022] | Series: The Greenwood Press daily life through history series | Includes bibliographical references and index.
Identifiers: LCCN 2021032128 (print) | LCCN 2021032129 (ebook) | ISBN 9781440870132 (hardcover) | ISBN 9781440870149 (ebook)
Subjects: LCSH: Women—Egypt—History. | Women—Egypt—Social conditions. | Women—History—To 500. | Egypt—Civilization—To 332 B.C. | Egypt—History—To 332 B.C.
Classification: LCC HQ1137.E3 S23 2022 (print) | LCC HQ1137.E3 (ebook) | DDC 305.40962—dc23
LC record available at https://lccn.loc.gov/2021032128
LC ebook record available at https://lccn.loc.gov/2021032129

ISBN: 978-1-4408-7013-2 (print)
       978-1-4408-7014-9 (ebook)

26 25 24 23 22   1 2 3 4 5

This book is also available as an eBook.

Greenwood
An Imprint of ABC-CLIO, LLC

ABC-CLIO, LLC
147 Castilian Drive
Santa Barbara, California 93117
www.abc-clio.com

This book is printed on acid-free paper ∞

Manufactured in the United States of America

CONTENTS

PREFACE

Our modern knowledge of ancient Egyptian civilization has been greatly helped by the fact that the hot, dry climate of Egypt has preserved many objects and written documents. Also, because temples and tombs were built to last for eternity, they were constructed out of stone blocks, and as a result, many of them—although damaged—still stand. That said, temples and tombs reflect the state and the royal rulers and elite officials who built them. On the walls of these structures are carved and painted scenes that present a perfect, everlasting picture of the king and his land. Such idealized pictures hardly represent everyday life in ancient Egypt. It has to be pointed out that royalty and the elite made up a very small tip of the enormous pyramid of ancient Egyptian society, and because the king and his officials were all male, their view of life would only represent 50% of ancient Egypt anyway.

The study of Egyptology is heavily based on documents, of which many remain, not only on papyrus but also inscribed on the walls of temples and tombs. From what is known of the ancient Egyptian educational system, all schooling was for boys, to train them to be scribes and to grow up and work for the state. This discussion may seem like a digression on masculine domination in ancient Egypt, but it is important to understand why there should be a book on the daily life of women in ancient Egypt and why it is so difficult to actually write a book like that.

Around the 1980s, when archaeologists in general realized that the understanding of the past was primarily based on a male past, the reaction of some to make up for the lack of a holistic approach to ancient societies was "put in a woman and stir." Hopefully, this approach will not appear in this book, although it is difficult to avoid it. Many topics such as kingship, the military, and administrative structure may seem to have been left out, but if a topic did not include women or there was no information relevant about women in it, it was not included in this book. That said, the author does provide substantially more information about elite women than non-elite women, but there was no real way to escape that. Elite and royal women had titles inscribed on stone monuments and had stone-built tombs or space in their husbands' tombs, so scholars simply have more evidence about them. It must be pointed out, however, that this evidence may not reflect daily life, but again, eternal life in the afterlife.

A typical village woman would have worked hard, possibly suffered horribly in childbirth, cooked, cleaned, and raised children. When she died, at the age of twenty-five to thirty years, she would have been buried in a pit dug in the village cemetery, perhaps wrapped in a reed bundle with a bead necklace and possibly a small amulet or a vessel or two of food or drink. An archaeologist finding her burial would note the few objects present and how they compare to others in similar and contemporary cemeteries. The osteologist who studies her skeleton might note the skeletal changes in her toes, knees, and some of the vertebrae and conclude that she spent time grinding grain for bread and beer. A healed fracture of her left arm shows that someone in the village was a healer and put a proper splint on her arm. Her teeth would be worn down and several lost, which is to be expected when one eats bread that sand gets into. In other words, this woman was a very typical lower-class or lower-middle-class housewife, but what else can we learn about her? What about her dreams, thoughts, and likes or dislikes? What was her daily routine like? Very little about a typical woman's life in ancient Egypt can be figured out, especially from the perspective of a modern mind deciding how an ancient person thought. These gaps in our knowledge are the reason why evidence from texts and artistic depictions, which are products of a mostly elite life, have to be depended on for information.

This book is broken into seven chapters, the topics of which often overlap. For example, discussing a priestess belongs in the chapter on religion, but as she is also paid for what she does as a priestess, the topic appears in the chapter on work as well. Each chapter starts out with a brief historical fiction paragraph based on ancient evidence, and at the end of select chapters, there is a short translation of a primary source to give readers an idea about how ancient Egyptians presented themselves.

Chapter One is titled "Society and Family Life" and covers family structure, marriage and divorce, motherhood, children and childbirth, the elderly, and widows. Chapter Two is concerned with "Work, Economy, and Law," focusing on priestesses, weaving, crime, and punishment. Chapter Three, "Literacy, Education, and Health," discusses female literacy and schooling, as well as health problems and how they were treated. Chapter Four on "Personal Property" covers a range of topics, including houses, furniture, cooking, cosmetics, clothing, and pets.

Chapter Five broadly covers the topic of "Entertainment" by discussing music, song, dance, drinking, games, toys, and love poetry. "The Life of Royal Women" is covered in Chapter 6, presenting the various female members of the royal family and their status and titles, the harem, and descriptions of the lives of famous queens such as Nefertari and Hatshepsut. The last chapter, Chapter Seven, "Religious Life and the Afterlife," examines expressions of religiosity in daily life, important goddesses, the concept of the afterlife, mummification, the funeral, the tomb, ancestral cults, and the "wise woman."

In the Introduction, a map has been provided so that readers can see the various places in Egypt discussed in the text. In particular, check the map for the locations of four important villages and towns that have supplied a large percentage of the material covered in the book: Lahun, Wah-Sut, Amarna Workmen's Village, and perhaps the most important, the workmen's village of Deir el-Medineh. A glossary will help with the meaning of ancient Egyptian words and Egyptological terms. At the back of the book is an overall bibliography of excellent and readable books about ancient Egypt, followed by specific bibliographies for each chapter.

INTRODUCTION

This introduction is planned to be a quick and easily digested overview of ancient Egyptian history so that the topics in the book, which all focus on the life of women, can be more easily understood in a broader context. Keeping straight the periods and dynasties of ancient Egypt can be somewhat challenging at the beginning, and this historical introduction along with the timeline should help make the basic scope of ancient Egyptian history clear. Pharaonic Egypt is quite a long history, roughly three thousand years—if not the longest, then certainly one of the longest-lasting human cultures on the earth. The ancient Egyptian language, with all of its dialects through time, is accepted as the longest-lasting language. This enormous span of time is something to keep in mind, as it is too easy to conflate everything ancient Egyptian together.

This historical overview is purposely more detailed in covering the three most important periods of ancient Egyptian history: the Old Kingdom, the Middle Kingdom, and the New Kingdom. The word "kingdom" is applied to the long periods in which Egypt was one unified state ruled by one king. These three kingdoms are the periods of ancient pharaonic civilization that are focused on in this book, and therefore, to be most helpful to the reader, these periods are also stressed in this compact historical description.

Ancient Egypt as a state with one ruling king formed about 3300 BCE out of two predynastic cultures, the Nagada culture in

ANCIENT EGYPT

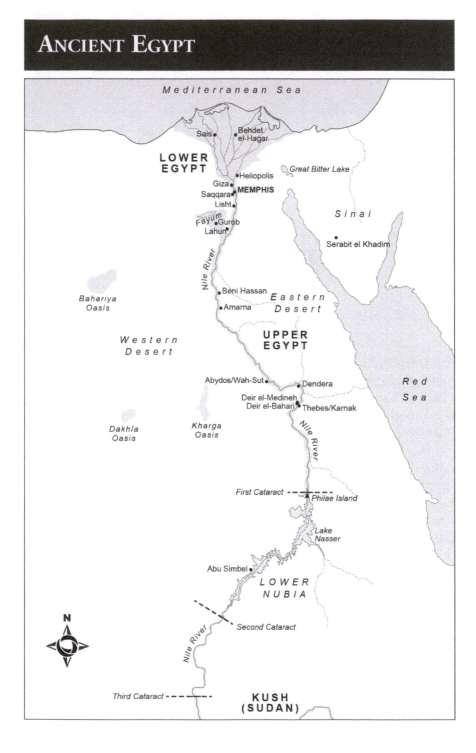

Mediterranean Sea

Sais•
Behdet
el-Hagar•

**LOWER
EGYPT**

Great Bitter Lake

•Heliopolis

Giza•
Saqqara•   **MEMPHIS**
Lisht•

S i n a l

Fayum
•Gurob
Lahun•

Serabit el Khadim•

*Bahariya
Oasis*

•Beni Hassan

*E a s t e r n
D e s e r t*

•Amarna

*W e s t e r n
D e s e r t*

**UPPER
EGYPT**

Nile River

Abydos/Wah-Sut•

•Dendera

*R e d
S e a*

*Dakhla
Oasis*

*Kharga
Oasis*

Deir el-Medineh•
Deir el-Bahari•   •Thebes/Karnak

Nile River

First Cataract - - - - -
•Philae Island

*Lake
Nasser*

Abu Simbel•

*L O W E R
N U B I A*

N

Nile River

Second Cataract

Third Cataract - - - - -   **KUSH
(SUDAN)**

Upper Egypt, based at the sites of Hierakonpolis and Abydos, and the Maadi-Buto culture, based in the delta at those two main sites. The process of unification to become a state is not entirely clear, but it was probably a slow, gradual spread of Upper Egyptian material culture and political power into Lower Egypt rather than a military conquest. It was not clear until relatively recently that there were kings of Egypt, ruling a large, single state before the time of the traditional beginning of ancient Egyptian history with the First Dynasty. The First Dynasty had been accepted as the beginning of the Egyptian state, and with the evidence of the Narmer Palette showing the king triumph, Narmer had been accepted as the conqueror and first king of Egypt.

Egyptologists now refer to the period of predynastic unification as Dynasty Zero, to stress it is before the First Dynasty, and accept Narmer as the last king of Dynasty Zero. The kings of this dynasty made their capital at Memphis but were buried at Abydos in an area called Umm el-Ga'ab. In Tomb Uj, the largest tomb in this cemetery, the earliest hieroglyphic writing on small bone labels was found. The area just south of the Dynasty Zero tombs became the most important royal burial ground of the First and Second Dynasties that followed, although three kings of the Second Dynasty were buried at Saqqara. There is evidence that one queen in the First Dynasty, named Meretneith, served as regent and ruled for her son, King Den, when her husband, King Djet, had died. Although Meretneith only held the title "King's mother," not the title "king," she had a tomb in the same cemetery as all the other kings of the First and Second Dynasties.

These kings at Abydos had funerary complexes, with two different parts in different places. At the desert area called Umm el-Ga'ab, the tombs themselves were square burial chambers down in the ground, with a mastaba, a rectangular bench-like superstructure covering it on the surface. Then, farther to the east at the edge of cultivation, each king built a large mudbrick enclosure, often referred to as a "funerary fort," as a space for his cult and ritual celebrations. These structures are located very near the Osiris temple at Abydos and must have been considered a space for the king parallel to that of the god.

The next dynasty, the Third, begins the period known as the Old Kingdom, or the Pyramid Age. The best-known king of this dynasty, King Djoser, builds his Step Pyramid Complex at Saqqara, which is both a development out of the funeral architecture at Abydos and a remarkable change from it. His complex began with a rectangular enclosure just like a funerary fort with a mastaba covering a very deep burial chamber. Additions were then made to the sides and top of the mastaba until it had become a pyramid with six steps on each side. There may have been a religious meaning behind the architecture, as a later Pyramid Text spell says to the king that "a stairway has been constructed for you, that you may ascend to heaven."

The Step Pyramid Complex was built out of limestone, not mudbrick, making it the earliest known completely stone monument. It has a number of new architectural elements added into its plan. On the north side of the pyramid is what might be a copy of the king's palace in stone, which served as a funerary temple, along with a serdab, a small, closed room, with a *ka*-statue of the king on the east side. There is a very large open court for some of the rituals of the king's *heb sed*, a celebration that took place after thirty years of rule. The point of the ritual was to renew and legitimize the king's rule for yet another thirty years and so on for eternity. On the south side of the court is a separate small and deep burial chamber, referred to as the south tomb. Perhaps it was for the king's *ka* or soul? Scholars do not really know. On the east side of the court are chapels for all the gods and goddesses of Egypt to come and watch the king be crowned during the *heb sed*, once with the Red Crown of Lower Egypt and once with the White Crown of Upper Egypt.

All these spaces in the Step Pyramid Complex and their functions are for the king's soul, for his afterlife. This is not the complex of a human king on the earth but for a divine king who died but will be reborn forever in the afterlife. The complex has combined what was needed by a living king, such as a palace and a *heb sed* court, with the needs of a deceased king, such as a burial chamber and a place to offer food to his *ka*, or soul, so that he would continue to live forever. On the east side of the Step Pyramid were also shaft tombs for the king's family members.

With the Fourth Dynasty, kings build true pyramids set in a completely different kind of complex, which reflects a shift to the importance of the cult of the sun god in both the king's life and afterlife. The true pyramid served as a sunray ramp for the king's ascension to heaven, and the alignment of all the structures of the true pyramid complex was designed on an east-to-west axis, following the sun's rising and setting. The importance of the sun cult increases, and by the Fifth Dynasty, every king builds not only a pyramid complex but also a sun temple. Scholars have put forth various opinions on the meaning of these sun temples. Clearly, sun temples stress the relationship of the king with the sun god, Ra, and his wife, the goddess Hathor, but they also seem to be tied to the *heb sed* and the renewal of royal legitimacy.

At the very end of the Fifth Dynasty, Pyramid Texts appear on the walls of the burial chamber in the pyramid of King Unas at Saqqara. The point of these spells is to protect the king and help him into the afterlife. The emphasis in the texts is on the god Osiris, because his death and resurrection are the model for that of the king, although both the gods, Ra and Osiris, are part of rebirth and eternal life. Pyramid Texts continued to be used in Sixth Dynasty pyramids for both kings and queens, but their use stops with the end of the Old Kingdom.

The Sixth Dynasty seems to have had political problems within the royal family, as King Tety may have been assassinated, and after that, one of the queens in the harem was investigated for conspiring against the following king, Pepy I. There is some evidence for a co-regency of Pepy I and his son Merenra, and if so, it would be the earliest known co-regency in the ancient Egyptian royal line. What happened in a co-regency is that the king would have his oldest son made king along with him so that if he died, there was a king already ruling. In this way, the royal family could protect their hold on the throne. At the end of the Sixth Dynasty, King Pepy II took the throne as a young boy, and so his mother, Queen Ankhenespepy II, ruled as regent for him. Pepy II is often given credit for his ninety-year reign, but more likely, his reign probably lasted sixty years. Little is known about the Old Kingdom after this, although it lasts, centered at the ancient city of Memphis until the end of the Eighth Dynasty.

By this point, climate change, which had begun in the later Fifth Dynasty, had turned the savannas on each side of the Nile valley into the deserts that they are today. Wildlife vanished or moved farther south, and plant life died. Tomb inscriptions of this time speak of drought and famine. Particularly in Upper Egypt, nomarchs took control and tried to take care of the people in their nome or province. Eventually civil war broke out between a ruling line at Heracleopolis, just south of the Fayum, and rulers at Thebes in Upper Egypt. This period, known as the First Intermediate Period, lasted from the Seventh Dynasty through to the later part of the Eleventh Dynasty.

By both military and political pressure, Mentuhotep II of the later Eleventh Dynasty reunited Egypt and ruled as sole king, beginning the period known as the Middle Kingdom. His center of rule remained at Thebes, and he was buried there as well, in the mountain against which he built his funerary temple. To stress his legitimacy, Mentuhotep II followed many Old Kingdom policies, such as marrying his sister and stressing his divinity from his mother, the goddess Hathor, wife of the sun god. In fact, where he built his funerary temple was the site of a cult of Hathor.

Mentuhotep II's reign over a united Egypt began the period of the Middle Kingdom, which lasts through the end of the Thirteenth Dynasty. Amenemhat I, the first king of the Twelfth Dynasty, may have been a vizier who usurped the throne, but after ruling for thirty years, he was assassinated. Amenemhat had left Thebes and built a new royal residence at a city named Itja-tawy, probably near Lisht south of Memphis, where the king built his pyramid. The king's badly damaged pyramid has been excavated, but the city of Itja-tawy has never been found. He was followed by his son Senusret I, who reigned over a time of extensive temple building, cutting of statuary, and writing of literary works. Much of all of this art and writing was propaganda about being loyal to the king. This family dynasty started by Amenemhat I lasted two hundred years, handing the throne down from father to son, until the last king of the dynasty was a queen named Sobekneferu. Scholars assume that she was the daughter of a king and also was married to one, but there is no clear evidence. She seems to have had a short reign of three to four years. Several headless statues of Sobekneferu have been found. She is wearing a female dress, with the kilt of a pharaoh worn over it.

The kings of the Twelfth Dynasty returned to the building of true pyramids, although almost all were built of brick and then cased only in stone, not built all in stone. These pyramid complexes also do not follow the rather rigid plan of the pyramid complex running from east to west seen in the Old Kingdom. The Middle Kingdom pyramid builders were very concerned with the pyramid being robbed, hid the actual entrance, and had fake shafts and chambers, hidden passageways, and massively heavy stone slabs over the king's sarcophagus, none of which was successful in the end in keeping robbers away.

Another type of architecture that was predominant in the Middle Kingdom was the building of fortresses south of Egypt. The southern border of ancient Egypt was at the First Cataract of the Nile. South of this point was the land of Nubia. Lower Nubia was the area between the First and Second Cataracts, while Upper Nubia was south of that and included the area of the Third Cataract and up to the Fourth. These cataracts on the Nile were places in which granite broke up the river interfering with travel by boat. The people of Lower Nubia, referred to by modern archaeologists as the C-people during the time of the Middle Kingdom, had a close and fairly friendly trading relationship with Egypt. Nubia was especially important to Egypt for its gold mines and for supplying exotic goods from farther south in Africa. But the Kerma people, who established an urban center above the Third Cataract, began to pose a threat to Egypt's control over Nubia. Under King Senusret I, Egypt began building forts in Lower Nubia, and under the later king Senusret III, a string of forts was completed down to the Second Cataract.

The Thirteenth Dynasty, the last dynasty of the Middle Kingdom, had a stable government administration, but it slowly lost control over the country, partially because of the infiltration of a great number of people from Syro-Palestine who settled for the most part in the delta, where an Egyptian town named Avaris became an Asiatic city. Finally, the rulers of these people arrived, called the Hyksos by the later Greeks, based on the ancient Egyptian name, *heka hasut*, and they established control over Lower Egypt. Six Hyksos kings are known, and they formed the Fifteenth Dynasty of Egypt. The Hyksos brought with them new warfare technology that the Egyptians did not yet have, which would become essential in the military of Egypt's New Kingdom to come: the horse and chariot and the composite bow.

Eventually a new family of rulers emerged in Thebes and began the struggle against the Hyksos in the north. These Thebans are the kings of the Seventeenth Dynasty. The Hyksos had established a trade relationship with the people of Kerma that went through the Western Desert, going around the Egyptians established at Thebes. The Egyptians captured a letter going from the Hyksos to the king of Kerma, saying that the Hyksos would move south, and the Kerma people should move north, and the two of them would defeat the Egyptians and share the land of Egypt between them. When King Kamose in Thebes read this letter, he moved north and defeated the Egyptian allies of the Hyksos in northern Upper Egypt and then launched the first Egyptian attack on the city of Avaris. His brother Ahmose, who followed him on the throne, was successful in forcing the Hyksos out of the delta and pursued them into southern Palestine, destroying their allied city of Sharuhen. This victory begins the period of the New Kingdom, with King Ahmose ruling over a reunited single state of Egypt.

Undoubtedly, the Hyksos invasion of Egypt served as the justification for Egypt to move north militarily into the countries of the Levant. A new requirement of the king in the New Kingdom became "to extend the boundaries of Egypt," and so the kings set out to control an empire in the north in the area of Palestine, Lebanon, and Syria, as well as to rebuild and occupy the forts in Nubia. King Thutmose I began military campaigns in both the north and the south, and his grandson King Thutmose III completed the building of the empire to Syria in the north and the Fifth Cataract in the south. The god Amun-Ra of Karnak Temple was the patron deity of the empire and the protector of the king in battle. Booty from captured Levantine cities, such as that of Megiddo, poured into the temple. Thebes became the most important religious center in Egypt, associated also with the fact that kings were now buried in the Valley of the Kings, behind the Theban mountain, and their large funerary temples were out on the plain in front of the mountain, across the river from Karnak Temple.

Thutmose III became king when he was still an infant, and so his stepmother, Queen Hatshepsut, served as the regent for him, as his physical mother was not a member of the royal family. After several years, Hatshepsut proclaimed herself king along with him, and they ruled together in a co-regency for twenty-two years, until Hatshepsut passed away. The damage to Hatshepsut's monuments was not carried out until some twenty years after her death when Thutmose III was preparing to make his own son, Amenhotep II, co-regent with him and, for reasons still not completely clear, wanted to remove evidence of Hatshepsut's family line.

Somewhat later, under King Amenhotep III, the cult of the sun god and the king's importance as the son of the sun grew substantially. Amenhotep III deified himself as the sun god and his wife, Queen Tiye, as the goddess Hathor, wife of the sun god. After a thirty-four-year rule over a peaceful and enormously wealthy Egypt, his son, Amenhotep IV, who changed his name to Akhenaten, left Thebes in year five of his reign, after closing the temple of Amun. Akhenaten moved much farther north and built a city at Amarna for his form of the sun god, Aten, the physical disk of the sun. Twelve years later, Akhenaten died, and within three years, the city of Amarna was abandoned. Under Tutankhamun and the kings Ay and Horemheb following him, Egyptian religion reverted back to what was considered standard state religion.

With the death of the childless King Horemheb, Ramses I, his general, took the throne, starting the Nineteenth Dynasty, but died shortly thereafter. His son, Seti I, proclaimed himself the "Bringer of the Renaissance" and carried out numerous military expeditions as well as an extensive building program. His son was Ramses II, one of the longest ruling kings of Egypt with a reign of sixty-seven years. Ramses II battled the Hittites from ancient Anatolia and then, much later, signed a peace treaty with them and eventually married a Hittite princess. Ramses II deified himself as the god Ra in his temple at Abu Simbel and deified his wife, Nefertari, as Hathor in the smaller temple that he made there for her. His son, King Merneptah, who finally succeeded him on the throne had to deal with a large invasion from Libya. The end of the Nineteenth Dynasty, as well as the beginning of the next dynasty, the Twentieth, is not well understood but included the reign of a queen named Tausret taking the throne for a period of probably eight years.

The best-known king of the Twentieth Dynasty is Ramses III who fought not only a battle with the Libyans, like Merneptah, but also a large invasion of migrating people known as the Sea Peoples who came from farther north, perhaps the area of modern Eastern Europe. Egypt's empire in the north was lost at this time, and little is known about Egypt's presence in Nubia to the south. Ramses III was assassinated in a harem conspiracy; a recent CT scan of this king's mummy showed that his throat was cut. The later part of the Twentieth Dynasty suffered from economic problems and civil war, along with seemingly short periods of rule, by kings all named Ramses, from Ramses IV to Ramses XI. This period ended with the High Priests of Amun ruling in Thebes and up to the city of El-Hibeh, south of the Fayum, while the king stayed in the royal residence of Ramses in the delta and ruled Lower Egypt. This situation brings about the Third Intermediate Period.

Because of the constant migration of Libyans settling in the delta, Dynasties Twenty-One to Twenty-Four were all ruled by Libyan kings. The Twenty-Fourth Dynasty based at the delta town of Sais was perhaps the most aggressive in wanting to expand control south to Thebes, such that the Kushites in the Sudan, centered at the Fourth Cataract, heard of this and moved north to protect Egypt, and Karnak Temple in particular, as they were loyal to the cult of the god Amun. All the Libyan kings eventually surrendered to the Kushites, who then ruled over Egypt as the Twenty-Fifth Dynasty. The Kushites were chased out of Egypt in 664 BCE by the

Assyrians from northern Mesopotamia, who added Egypt to their empire. From now on, in the period called the Late Period of Egyptian history, Egypt will have short periods of independence, mixed with two periods of belonging to the Persian Empire, before Egypt is taken over by Alexander the Great in 332 BCE, beginning Greek rule over Egypt, and ending the pharaonic period.

TIMELINE OF EVENTS

This timeline gives the dates of the most important periods and dynasties of ancient Egyptian history, until the time that Alexander the Great takes Egypt from the Persians and the Ptolemaic period begins. For each period, the most important characteristics or events are pointed out. Whenever possible, important evidence about ancient Egyptian women is included.

5300 BCE: **Predynastic Period**	People begin to settle down in the Nile valley, domesticating plants and animals, and beginning to produce pottery. The Nagada material culture is important in Upper Egypt, while Maadi-Buto material culture is important in the delta. Most of the archaeological material from this period is from cemeteries.
3200 BCE: **Dynasty Zero**	The predynastic cultures of Egypt unify into one state with a capital at Memphis. The country is ruled by a king who is considered to be divine, as he is Horus, the falcon god. The earliest hieroglyphic writing is found in Tomb Uj at Abydos. King Narmer rules as the last king of this period.

3000 BCE:
Early Dynastic
Period

This period consists of Dynasties One and Two. Memphis is the capital of Egypt. Royal tombs are built at both Abydos and Saqqara. The king's mother, Meretneith, rules as the regent for her young son, King Den. The title of king's wife appears for the first time.

2686 BCE:
Old Kingdom

This period consists of Dynasties Three to Eight. Kings are buried in pyramids at Dahshur, Giza, Saqqara, and Abu Sir. The first pyramid is the Step Pyramid at Saqqara, and after that, true pyramids with smooth sides are built. Many women hold the title of Priestess of Hathor. Kings of the Fifth Dynasty build sun temples. Pyramid Texts begin to be inscribed in royal pyramids at the end of the Fifth Dynasty. Queen Ankhenes-pepy II rules as the regent for her young son, Pepy II, in the Sixth Dynasty.

2160 BCE:
First Intermediate
Period

This period consists of Dynasties Nine to late Eleven. Egypt is no longer unified under one king, and provincial rulers take over power. Climate change creates deserts on each side of the river, and Nile inundations are erratic at times. Societal changes seem to affect the independence and economic freedom of women, which is evidenced in the disappearance of titles they held in the Old Kingdom. Egypt is reunited by King Mentuhotep II in the late Eleventh Dynasty. The cult of the goddess Hathor is important at this time.

2055 BCE:
Middle Kingdom

This period consists of the later Eleventh Dynasty ruling from Thebes, followed by the Twelfth and Thirteenth Dynasties ruling from a new royal residence at Itja-tawy, north of the Fayum. Kings once again build true pyramids for their burials. The most common woman's title is now "mistress of the house"; the title of "priestess" has largely disappeared. A queen named Sobekneferu rules as the last king of the Twelfth Dynasty; among other titles, she calls herself the "female Horus." The towns of Lahun in the Fayum and Wah-Sut at Abydos become important provincial centers.

1650 BCE: Second Intermediate Period

This period consists of Dynasties Fifteen to Seventeen. The Hyksos from Syro-Palestine take over and rule the delta. Egyptian kings rule at Thebes, and eventually King Ahmose chases the Hyksos back out of the delta and reunites Egypt. Royal females gain political and religious importance and are active participants in their husbands' reigns. The position of God's Wife of Amun is established.

1550 BCE: New Kingdom

This period consists of Dynasties Eighteen to Twenty. Egypt creates an empire in Syro-Palestine to the north and to the south in Nubia and the Sudan. The kings are buried in the Valley of the Kings at Thebes, and the village of Deir el-Medineh is established for the workmen who cut and decorate these tombs. The god Amun in the Temple of Karnak is considered to be the divine father of the king and the patron deity of the Egyptian empire. In the Eighteenth Dynasty, Hatshepsut rules as king in a co-regency with her stepson Thutmose III. King Akhenaten builds the city of Amarna, which also has a workmen's village. In the Nineteenth Dynasty, Queen Nefertari is deified as Hathor in the small temple of Abu Simbel and has a beautiful tomb in the Valley of the Queens. In the Twentieth Dynasty, King Ramses III is assassinated in a harem conspiracy.

1069 BCE: Third Intermediate Period

This period consists of Dynasties Twenty-One to Twenty-Four. Egypt is now ruled by kings in the north and the High Priests of Amun in the south. The Valley of the King is no longer used. The population in the north has become increasingly Libyan. Female chantresses become important in temple ritual, especially in Thebes. A temple complex for the god Amun is built in the delta at Tanis where royal tombs are also built.

747 BCE: Twenty-Fifth Dynasty

A line of kings from the Sudan, devoted to the cult of Amun, comes north and reunites Egypt by defeating the Libyan kings in the delta. They rule in Egypt but are buried in a small pyramid in the area of the Fourth Cataract. The God's Wife of Amun holds power in the city of Thebes, which is sacked by the Assyrians in 664 BCE, when they are pursuing the Sudanese kings south and out of Egypt.

664 BCE: Late Period

This last period of pharaonic power consists of Dynasties Twenty-Six to Thirty-One. Egyptian kings struggle to stay independent using Greek mercenaries. The cult of the goddess Isis becomes important, and her temple at Philae at the First Cataract is a focus of pilgrimages. The Persians rule Egypt in Dynasties Twenty-Seven and Thirty-One. The Thirtieth Dynasty, in particular, was a time of massive temple building. Alexander the Great takes Egypt from the Persians in 332 BCE, beginning the Greek or Ptolemaic Period in Egypt.

Source: This timeline is based on the chronology given in Ian Shaw (ed.). 2000. *The Oxford History of Ancient Egypt*. Oxford: Oxford University Press.

GLOSSARY

This glossary contains terms that are used in Egyptology, as well as names of locations that were important in ancient Egypt and names of gods and goddesses who may not have been explained in the text.

Abu Simbel: A site in Nubia where King Ramses II constructed two temples, one for himself as the sun god and another for his queen, Nefertari, as the goddess Hathor.

Akh: A spirit, someone who has died and lives again in the afterlife.

Amarna: A site where King Akhenaten built a city dedicated to his god, the Aten.

Ammit: A frightening creature who gobbles up the heart of the deceased if it is heavy with sin when weighed on scales in the judgment to enter the afterlife.

Ba: One of five important aspects of a person. The *ba* is depicted as a bird and leaves the tomb in the daytime, returning to the body at night.

Bastet: The cat goddess who was worshipped at Bubastis in the delta. Bastet was a goddess of the household, women, and children.

Bes: An ugly dwarf who protected children and women in childbirth.

Book of the Dead: A collection of funerary spells that were used beginning with the New Kingdom.

Canopic jars: Four jars that held the lungs, stomach, liver, and intestines when they were removed during mummification.

Cartouche: An oval rope that was put around the names of kings, and later queens, for protection.

Co-regency: When two people, usually an older father and his son, rule together as two kings so that if one dies, the other is already ruling and the throne cannot be seized by anyone else.

Deir el-Medineh: The workmen's village on the West Bank of Thebes where the men lived who cut and painted the tombs in the Valley of the Kings and the Valley of the Queens.

Faience: A fired ceramic made mostly of silica, most often colored blue. It was used for many objects, such as scarabs, beads, and rings.

False door: An imitation doorway set inside a tomb for the spirit of the deceased to pass through and receive offerings.

Fayum A: An archaeological name for people who settled in the Fayum around 5000 BCE.

Hathor: A very important goddess who was the wife of the sun god. She could take the form of a cow. Hathor was the goddess of women and childbirth, as well as love, dancing, and drinking.

Hatti: An Egyptian name for the land of the Hittites in ancient Turkey.

Heart scarab: A scarab that was placed over the heart, inscribed with Spell 30b of the Book of the Dead, to keep the heart from revealing any sin the deceased was guilty of.

Heket: A frog-headed goddess of fertility who helped protect childbirth.

Hieratic: The handwritten cursive form of hieroglyphs.

Hieroglyphs: The script of the ancient Egyptian language that consisted of signs that had either phonetic or pictorial value. The most important signs were the twenty-six that made up the alphabet.

Horus: The falcon god, son of Osiris and Isis, who took the throne when Osiris was killed. Every king of Egypt was "Horus on the throne of the living."

Hsyt: The Egyptian title for a "singer."

Hyksos: Refers to the leaders of people from Syro-Palestine who had settled in the Egyptian delta during the later Middle Kingdom. The Hyksos ruled from the town of Avaris during the period known as Dynasty Fifteen.

Ipt: The word for the royal harem in the Old Kingdom.

Isis: Wife of Osiris and mother of Horus. She was a very important mother goddess during the Late Period and throughout Graeco-Roman times.

Ka: The *ka* is a person's soul. It was created with you, and when you die, the *ka* has to continue to be taken care of.

Kap: The part of the royal harem where the royal children lived.

Kenbet: This is the name of a local law court. The village of Deir el-Medineh had its own *kenbet* to decide cases and problems at the village.

Khener: The name of dance groups who are the followers of the goddess Hathor.

Khnum: The ram god who created people and their souls on a potter's wheel.

Khonsu: The moon god and son of Amun and Mut. His temple was at Karnak in the southwest corner of the enclosure.

Lahun: A town in the Fayum that began as the site of the pyramid of King Senusret II of the Twelfth Dynasty and later became an important provincial center.

Maat: This is the concept of justice and order. The king's duty is to uphold *maat*.

Mastaba: A private tomb built out of limestone blocks in the shape of a bench.

Mehen: The name of a board game.

Mena nesut: The title given to a male tutor of royal children.

Menat: A heavy bead necklace held by priestesses of the goddess Hathor.

Menat nesut: The title held by a wet nurse for a royal child.

Meskhenet: The four bricks that a woman squatted on to give birth; also, the name of the goddess of childbirth.

Mitanni: The Egyptian name for an ancient country in the area of northern Syria.

Mwt: The ancient Egyptian word for mother as well as vulture. The goddess Mut was the wife of Amun of Karnak Temple.

Natron: A compound of sodium carbonate and sodium bicarbonate that was put on bodies to remove water and fat during mummification.

Nebet per: This is the title of housewife, "mistress of the house," which first appears in the Middle Kingdom.

Neith: An old goddess, possibly of war, who became important again in the Late Period, with a temple at Sais in the delta.

Neolithic: The term that refers to an early human culture that has settled down, plants crops and herds animals, as well as produces pottery.

Nephthys: The sister of Isis and Osiris, who helps Isis retrieve the body of Osiris and bury him.

Opening of the Mouth: The important ritual carried out at the funeral before the deceased is buried.

Osiris: The god of the afterlife. Osiris had ruled as king until killed by his jealous brother, Seth.

Ostracon: A flat piece of limestone or a pot sherd that is used to write on.

Ptah: A creator god whose cult temple was at Memphis, the capital of Egypt. Ptah was the patron deity of craftsmen and so was worshipped at the workmen's village of Deir el-Medineh.

Punt: The Egyptian name for a place along the southern Red Sea where they went to get myrrh and incense. The location is unknown.

Pyramid Texts: Religious spells that first appear in the pyramid of King Unas at the end of the Fifth Dynasty.

Ra: The sun god, creator of all life. The king functioned as the sun god on the earth.

Red Crown: The crown of Lower Egypt.

Renenutet: A cobra goddess associated with the harvest.

Sakhmet: The lioness goddess who brought plague and illness and was also the patron goddess of doctors.

Sau: The word for magician.

Scarab: An amulet in the shape of the scarab beetle that symbolized rebirth.

Sekhet Iaru: The Egyptian name for the "Field of Rushes," the location of the eternal afterlife.

Senet: The most popular board game in ancient Egypt.

Serdab: A hidden tomb chamber, often behind the false door, where a *ka*-statue of the deceased was placed.

Serekh façade: The panel design that was on the wall of the king's palace. It was also used to frame the king's Horus name, the first and oldest of the king's five names.

Serket: The scorpion goddess. She helped to protect the canopic jars.

Seshat: This is the word for female scribe and also the name of the goddess of writing.

Shemayit: This is the ancient Egyptian word for chantress.

Sistrum: A jingling instrument associated with the goddess Hathor and held by all chantresses.

Swnw: The ancient Egyptian word for doctor.

Ta rekhet: The ancient Egyptian word for wise woman.

Taweret: A goddess who protected pregnant women and babies. She was a mixture of a hippopotamus, crocodile, and lion.

Tyet: An amulet that seems to be a piece of cloth tied in a knot. It was a protective symbol of the goddess Isis.

Uraeus: This is the rearing cobra, and it is placed over the forehead of the king to protect him.

Valley of the Kings: The location of the royal tombs of the kings of the New Kingdom on the West Bank of Thebes.

Valley of the Queens: The location of the tombs of the queens of the New Kingdom on the West Bank of Thebes, south of the Valley of the Kings.

Vizier: The most important official under the king; he was also the highest judge in the land.

Wah-Sut: A Middle Kingdom town in south Abydos that was an important center in the Thirteenth Dynasty.

1

SOCIETY AND FAMILY LIFE

It was hot and dusty as she walked, leaning on her stick, back to the house at the end of the village. She and her husband, Khaemnun, now lived with Qenherkhopshef, one of their four sons, and his family. It was a crowded household, but their son would not have it any other way. "You never have to worry," he always said, "I will always take care of you." "I am so glad I finally did it," she thought. Without letting anyone in the house think she was doing anything but visit her daughter, Wosnakhte, at the beginning of the village, she had left the village and walked north to the village court. She had her will written out by the scribe of the court with five men as witnesses. She had made sure that it was clear. Her personal property was only to be inherited by four of her eight children. The other four, Neferhotep, Manenakhte, Henshene, and Khanub, would get nothing of hers. "They can inherit from their father," she scoffed, "but not from me." "They probably don't know if I am alive or dead," she said out loud, banging her stick down into the ground and scaring away one of the village dogs.

THE FAMILY

The unit of the family was, as in most cultures, the backbone of ancient Egyptian society. Evidence seems to show that most families were multigenerational, and the household consisted of parents and children along with grandparents, and often aunts. Sometimes it is confusing for modern scholars to figure out exact relationships in ancient Egyptian families because terms for family members from different generations were not distinguished. For example, the word used for son and grandson and daughter and granddaughter was the same. In the New Kingdom (1550–1069 BCE), a wife was often referred to with the word "sister," but it did not mean that the woman was actually physically related to her husband. There is some thought that the word "sister" first began to be used for a wife who was a man's cousin, and then, later in the New Kingdom, it simply became accepted as the word for wife.

Although brother-sister marriage is known among royalty in ancient Egypt, there is no evidence for sibling marriage outside of the royal family. As in ancient Egyptian mythology, gods married their sisters, such as the marriage of Osiris and Isis, both of whom were children of the earth god, Geb and his sister the sky goodness, Nut, it seems that sibling marriage was a sign of divinity, and kings chose it for that reason. Sibling marriage is also a way to keep power and property in the family, and that certainly played a part in ruling families. There is evidence for sibling marriages in the royal family in the Fourth Dynasty (2614–2494 BCE), the Eleventh and Twelfth Dynasties (2055–1773 BCE), and the Seventeenth and early Eighteenth Dynasties (1580–1279 BCE). There is not a clear pattern, but sibling marriage seems to occur at times when a new royal line begins and the kings need to stress their divine legitimacy to rule.

Archaeological evidence seems to show that the average ancient Egyptian household had six people. If a family was well-to-do, any number of servants lived with them as well.

Papyri found at the late Middle Kingdom (1877–1650 BCE) town of Lahun contain census information collected over a period of time, allowing a glimpse into the individuals who made up a household and how the character of the household changed (Kemp 2006: 219). The first document shows that a soldier named Hori lived in a house with his wife, Shepet, and their son, Sneferu. In the next document, this nuclear family of father, mother, and child is still in the same house, but they have been joined with the father's mother, Harekhni, and five other females who seem to have been the father's sisters. In the last document that refers to this household, Hori is not listed and so must have passed away, as his son Sneferu is now the head of the household. Sneferu's mother, Shepet, is still with him, as is his grandmother, Harekhni. Three of

Sneferu's five aunts are still part of the household, so two may have married or else died.

Another similar government census is known for the New Kingdom workmen's village at Deir el-Medineh on the West Bank of Thebes. It isn't clear why such a census was taken, but the village of Deir el-Medineh, like that of Lahun, belonged to the government, and they may have kept track of households to make sure that only people who were part of the workforce lived there. The Deir el-Medineh census papyrus is broken into fragments, but some parts are still readable. On the parts that can be read, none of the houses have as many as six inhabitants, and some houses only have the name of a single man as the inhabitant.

A fairly well-documented family is that of the farmer Heqanakht in the early reign of King Senusret I (1956–1911 BCE) of the Twelfth Dynasty. This family is documented not by a government census but by information in Heqanakht's personal letters. Heqanakht wrote a series of letters home to his family who lived in a settlement near the Fayum, when he was in Upper Egypt at Thebes. He had been made the *ka*-priest of an important official buried at Thebes, and so he had to be in Thebes for long periods of time. In the letters, which are mainly concerned with business and farming, various references are made to the members of his family and the family problems.

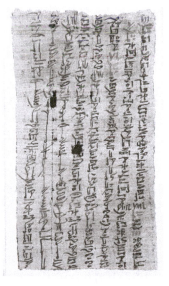

One of the letters sent by Heqanakht to his family in the early Middle Kingdom. It is written in hieratic script with black ink on papyrus. (The Metropolitan Museum of Art)

We learn from Heqanakht's accounts that on a monthly basis, he supported 18 people (Parkinson, 1991: 102). This group included his mother, Ipi; his second wife, Hepetet, whom he married recently; a son named Sneferu; another named Anpu; and at least one daughter, Neferet. Other males in the household may have been his brothers, sons of brothers, or men who worked with Heqanakht, but the relationships are not clear. There are also three female servants who live in the house. In the letters, it becomes clear that the new wife is not being treated well in the household, as at one point, Heqanakht asks, "What about this evil treatment of my new wife?" (Parkinson, 1991: 105). For some reason, Heqanakht seems to blame one of the female servants in the house, named Senen, for mistreating his wife. Heqanakht also mentions twice in the same letter that Sneferu should be well taken care of, so he must have been either the favorite son or perhaps the youngest.

MARRIAGE AND DIVORCE

Although the details involved in how people got married in ancient Egypt are not understood, it is clear from ancient Egyptian texts, known as wisdom literature, that getting married and starting a family were the societal ideals. Certainly, there must have been men and women who did not marry, although staying single seems to have been unusual. In the Lahun census discussed previously, it is clear that unmarried women stayed with their parents or brother and did not have a home of their own. There is some evidence in the Twelfth Dynasty that if a princess did not marry her brother, the king, then she did not marry. This would have been a rather strict way of keeping hold on the throne of Egypt. Women tended to be buried with their husband, and queens were buried by the pyramid of their husband, the king. A number of Twelfth Dynasty princess burials have been found, for example, near the Dashur pyramid of Amenemhat II and the Lahun pyramid of Senusret II. This placement of their tombs would indicate that these women never married and so were buried with their father, because they did not have a husband.

The word for marriage in ancient Egyptian was "establish a house," which is something that the man was supposed to do, and went hand in hand with having a family as well. Because the average life span in ancient Egypt would have been about twenty-five to thirty years, both women and men must have got married at a rather young age. Children would have been the expected outcome of marriage in ancient times, especially because there would not have been dependable contraceptives. There are, however, at least three ancient Egyptian medical texts that give "recipes" for "not to become pregnant" or "to cause a woman to stop pregnancy." In two of the texts, crocodile feces were to be mixed with dough and then soaked with something else, but the papyrus is damaged at that point. In the third papyrus, the "recipe" was to be a mixture of the pod from an acacia tree, colocynth, and dates, mixed with honey. Both of these mixtures were to be used as vaginal suppositories. The crocodile feces are the most unusual of the ingredients. Perhaps they had magical importance, because the crocodile was an animal associated with the god Seth, evil brother of the god Osiris, who wanted to stop Osiris's pregnant wife, Isis, from having a baby, because Seth, after having killed Osiris, wanted to take the throne and rule Egypt.

Outside of the royal family, marriages were monogamous and were expected to be lifelong. Kings could have any number of wives, perhaps in order to make sure that they had a son to follow them on the throne, but having more than one wife at a time does not seem to have been the case with nonroyal men. Divorce was known; it does not seem to have been looked down upon. Since a rather high number of women must have died in childbirth, it is not usual to find evidence in a tomb scene that shows a man with more than one wife, meaning that he had remarried after the death of the first wife. There is also written evidence that shows women who had been widowed married again.

Marriage was carried out privately, and there is no evidence of a religious or state ceremony, any official being present, or any particular document being signed. From the Late Period, beginning in 664 BCE and after, there are marriage contracts known that stipulated a sum of money, the "wife's gift," to be paid by the husband to the wife if he wanted to divorce her, but for the bulk of pharaonic civilization, there were no such documents known. There is some written evidence from the New Kingdom village of Deir el-Medineh that in order to ask to marry a woman, the man took a present to her parents. A marriage took place when the woman publicly moved in with the man. It appears that this relationship was meant to be long-lasting and that any children from the marriage inherited the property of their mother and father.

Divorce seems to have been much the same, in the sense of being carried out without any legal or religious intervention. The woman simply left the man's house and took her property with her. If there was an argument over personal or communal property, a divorce was decided in a local court, such as the court in the New Kingdom (1550–1069 BCE) village of Deir el-Medineh. There is written evidence that shows if the divorce was because of the wife's infidelity, she had to give up her claim to any communal property. If there was no disagreement that needed a court decision, the woman just moved out of her husband's house with her personal property, and the marriage ended. Evidence seems to show that a man was more likely to ask for a divorce than a woman and that the most common reasons given for a divorce were constant fighting, adultery, or that the man wanted to marry another woman, usually a younger one. There is no evidence at all from ancient Egypt as to what happened to the children when a couple divorced; it must have been clear to all involved as the matter of child custody was never written down.

CHILDREN AND CHILDBIRTH

Children in ancient Egypt were considered important because they would help their parents and take care of them in their old age. Parents also depended on their children to make sure that they had a proper burial when they died. There is no evidence whatsoever that ancient Egyptians preferred to have a boy rather than a girl when the baby was born. The only mention of the importance of having a son is found in the *Instructions of Any*, a text which is thought to have been written in the Eighteenth Dynasty of the New Kingdom (1550–1295 BCE). At the very beginning it says, "Take a wife while you're young, that she make a son for you" (Lichtheim 1976: 136). This advice probably fits with the tradition at that time that jobs, even government positions, were hereditary and went from father to son, keeping it within the family. Other ancient cultures—for example, the Greeks—preferred male children and exposed newly born females. The Greek historian Diodorus Siculus in 50 BCE wrote that the ancient Egyptians were very odd and "raise all their children" (Oldfather 1989: 275).

Another example of gender equality, when it comes to having boys or girls, is expressed in amuletic decrees of the Third Intermediate Period (1069–664 BCE). By means of an oracle, a god or goddess would pronounce that a female baby would be healthy and protected and, when she grew up and married, would have both male and female children. A similar pronouncement would be made for a male baby that he would be healthy and protected, and when he grew up and married, his wife would bear him both male and female children.

The ancient Egyptian idea that fertility is a characteristic of males, not females, may explain why ancient Egyptian men were accepting of whatever sex their children were. They were responsible for producing a girl or a boy, not their wife. Women were thought of as a container, so to speak. The seed for a child came from the father, who put it into the mother to be protected and taken care of until it was grown enough to be born. This idea of male fertility is behind all the creator myths of ancient Egypt; creators were all male: Atum or Ra, Amun (also Amun-Ra), and Ptah. One text, probably dating from the Sixth Dynasty of the Old Kingdom (2345–2181 BCE), known as the *Instructions of Ptahhotep*, gives some advice about how a man should take care of his son, if "by the grace of god" he has one: "Do for him all that is good, he is your son, your *ka* begot him, Don't withdraw your heart from him" (Lichtheim 1973: 66).

Ancient Egyptian medical papyri include directions for tests that could be done to see if a woman was able to have children and what sex the child would be. One test had a woman urinate on a bag of barley seeds and another bag full of emmer wheat seeds. If the seeds did not sprout, then the woman was not pregnant. If the seeds sprouted, then the test went one step further and stated that if the barley seeds sprouted, the woman would have a girl, and if the wheat sprouted, she would have a boy. This determination of the baby's sex was based on the fact that in the ancient Egyptian language, the word for barley was "feminine" and the word for wheat was "masculine," so it was hardly very accurate.

CHILDREN IN ANCIENT EGYPTIAN ART

Ancient Egyptian children were often depicted in tomb scenes and in statuary along with their parents. There were certain artistic characteristics, beyond just small size, in how a child was shown that made it clear that the individual was a child. They were normally shown nude, so perhaps children were often nude in daily life. Children also have their hair pulled into a sidelock on the right side of their head. Often an amulet in the shape of a fish hangs down from the sidelock. This amulet would have provided magical protection for the child if they fell into a canal, or the Nile River, that just like a fish they could swim; drowning must have been a very real danger in ancient Egypt. Children were also depicted holding their index finger up to their mouth, depicting a typical baby characteristic of sucking on fingers. In art, males were characteristically shown with red or brown skin, while women had white or yellow skin. These same colors were applied to boys and girls in painted scenes and statuary.

DIVINE PROTECTION FOR CHILDBIRTH

In ancient Egypt, as in other ancient civilizations, pregnancy and childbirth were extremely dangerous for both the mother and the child. As well, the first five years of a child's life could be dangerous in terms of survival, and ancient Egyptian women probably lost 50% of their children before the age of five. Certain deities, particularly Taweret and Bes, were called upon for protection. Taweret

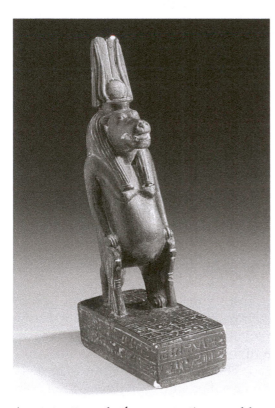

was a mix of a hippopotamus, lion, and crocodile. She was depicted as a hippopotamus, with a lion mane and paws and a crocodile tail. She was shown very round and heavy like a pregnant woman but was also very scary. Bes was a very ugly male dwarf, also mixed with lion characteristics. Both Taweret and Bes could be shown holding knives that made them even more fearsome. These two deities could be offered to at small shrines set up in the house, and they were also depicted on household objects and furniture used for children. In particular, Bes and Taweret were depicted on protective ivory wands that would be used to draw a circle

A statuette of the protective goddess Taweret, who is a hippopotamus with a lion head and crocodile tail. (Statue of Taweret, Cairo, Egypt, 1925–1933. Science Museum, London. Attribution 4.0 International (CC BY 4.0))

in the packed earth floor of the house, around the new mother and her baby. The magical protection of Taweret and Bes would then be around them and protect them from harm, especially since the wand was made from hippopotamus ivory, associating the protective wand even closer with the goddess Taweret.

There were other goddesses who were connected with the actual birth of the baby. It is known from ancient Egyptian texts that women squatted on "birth bricks" to raise them up off the ground in order to deliver their child. This allowed another woman who was helping her to catch and help deliver the baby. There were four bricks used, two horizontally stacked to support each foot. The "birth bricks" were related to a goddess named Meskhenet, who personified these bricks, and aided and protected the delivery of the baby. The name Meskhenet was also used for the actual bricks themselves.

In 2001, archaeologists discovered a birth brick for the first time, in an ancient Egyptian villa of the later Middle Kingdom (about 1650 BCE) at the town of Wah Sut in Abydos in Upper Egypt. The villa where the birth brick was found belonged to the governor of the town, and it is known that his wife was a princess. The

A magic ivory wand from the Middle Kingdom decorated with creatures who would protect women giving birth and children. (The Metropolitan Museum of Art)

brick was found in a section of the villa that seemed to have been a granary that was rebuilt into a seven-room domestic unit. Clay sealings were found there with the name of the "king's daughter, Reniseneb," and it is assumed that this unit was her private living area within her husband's large villa.

The brick was painted with religious and mythical images that likened the birth of the baby to the birth of the sun god, Ra, every morning and transferred divine protection to the child being born. The scenes on the Meskhenet also magically transformed the birthing mother into the goddess Hathor so that the mother herself became divine and protected at the moment of delivery. One long side of the brick was broken away, but the other side depicted a woman on a throne holding her newborn with two other women attending her. One stood behind her, and the other kneeled down in front of her with her arms out. This seems to suggest that the scene protects both the birth and just after. The four edges of the brick are somewhat damaged, but each had been painted with various protective creatures, such as Taweret, a lion, or a cobra, who would drive away or defeat anything evil or dangerous that would threaten the mother or the baby. These same creatures are those carved on the protective ivory wands just discussed previously.

We have no evidence for women who worked as midwives, although it seems logical that women with experience delivering babies would have been called upon to help out. There were doctors in ancient Egypt, but they were few and worked for elite and royal households. There were no specialties such as obstetrics or pediatrics, and in fact, any internal medical problem, such as a pregnancy, was dealt with using magic. Contrary to popular modern beliefs, the ancient Egyptians did not practice surgery, and there would have been no way to intervene and help a woman having difficulty delivering her baby, other than by using magical spells and objects.

Two objects were often kept in an ancient Egyptian house and were brought out in case of problems in labor or delivery. One was a small clay statue of the god Bes. It was used along with a magical spell that was to be recited four times over a dwarf of clay placed on the woman's abdomen. The main part of the spell was "Come down, placenta, come down, come down . . . she who is giving birth becomes better than she was, as if she was already delivered" (Janssen and Janssen 1990: 9). The second object was a small clay or limestone representation of a woman on a bed with a baby next to her. This piece would have been used in a similar magical fashion, called sympathetic magic, so that the woman in labor would become a happy, new mother with a healthy baby, just like the figure in the statuette.

DOMESTIC PROTECTION FOR MOTHERS AND THE NEWBORN

In about a third of the houses of the workmen's village at Deir el-Medineh, a special space was constructed in the first room of the house for the protection of the newborn baby. A rectangular brick platform, more than a meter long, was built against one of the walls, or in one of the corners, and was enclosed, sometimes all the way up to the ceiling. There was an opening in the middle of the long side, led up to by a short flight of steps. This structure has been called a bed or an altar. If it were a bed, it would only be comfortable for a baby, and it may well have been used as a protected space for one, particularly after birth. When these "beds" were discovered, some still had decoration on the outside. The decoration that remained depicted the god Bes, a protector of children and childbirth, or a female, dancing or playing a musical instrument. There were also leaves of the convolvulus, or morning glory, vine painted on some of the bed enclosures. This plant is also depicted growing on arbors, or other roofed but open spaces, where women are shown nursing their newborn babies. It is not yet clear, however, why this particular plant was associated with childbirth.

Actual wooden beds, referred to as "women's beds" in written documents from Deir el-Medineh, have been discovered at the village. The legs of the beds are carved in the shape of standing figures of the god Bes. The use for these beds is not completely clear, but it is thought that the mother and her newborn would sleep on it after the birth, with the Bes figure legs protecting them from harm. Since there is written evidence of someone in the village going to buy a birth amulet and a woman's bed, it does seem that there was a special protective bed to be used after childbirth.

BURIALS OF MOTHERS AND BABIES

In a late Middle Kingdom villa at Wah-Sut, called Building E by the excavators, five baby skeletons were found buried under the floor in the house; two of the babies had been placed in wooden boxes (Picardo 2006). All these burials were in the southwest portion of the villa, in what might have been the bedroom complex that belonged to the lady of the house. Four such burials were also found in contemporary palatial houses at the town of Lahun in the Fayum with one of the burials mentioned as being in a box. It seems that the mother must have wanted the baby close to her, so it was buried within the house and not in the village cemetery. The New Kingdom village of Deir el-Medineh has a hill running along its east side. Baby burials were found all along the bottom of the hill alongside the wall of the village. Again, it seems that keeping baby burials close to the family was of importance.

Sometimes skeletal evidence is found that shows both the mother and the baby must have died during the birth. The burial of Queen Mutnodjmet at Saqqara gives evidence of this sad occurrence. She was buried in the tomb of her husband, General Horemheb, who served under King Tutankhamun, and then eventually became king of Egypt himself. He may, in fact, have married Mudnod-jmet when he became king. Her skeleton shows that she was prob-ably thirty-five to forty years old at the time of her death. There are bones of a "mature fetus" mixed with her bones, suggesting that they both died during a difficult birth (Strouhal 2008: 1–4). Mutnodjmet's pubic bones also seem to suggest that she had suf-fered earlier difficult births, and the thickening seen in her skull vault might have been in reaction to extensive blood loss (Strouhal 2008: 3). Interestingly enough, this skeletal evidence may back up what scholars seem to know of the history at this time at the end of the Eighteenth Dynasty. King Horemheb (1323–1295 BCE) had no son to follow him on the throne, and so he picked another military man, Ramses I, as his successor.

POSTPARTUM CARE AND NAMING

We know very little about postpartum care in ancient Egypt, although there is some evidence that the woman and her child were secluded at least for the first two weeks. We do not understand if it was for protection in terms of health or some type of purification period. Breast feeding is depicted and mentioned in texts, and wet nurses are known as well, especially for royal children. We don't have any evidence that ancient Egyptians celebrated birthdays. It is not until the Middle Kingdom that we have some slight writ-ten evidence of individuals knowing in which king's reign they were born, and by the New Kingdom, we have a statement by the architect Amenhotep, son of Hapu, inscribed on his statue, that he is eighty years old. By the time of the Late Period beginning in 664 BCE, complete birth dates are known.

Children seem to have been named right at birth, and there is some evidence that it was the mother who chose the child's name. The name chosen either seemed to express something about the baby or the name was more formal and contained the name of a deity or reference to a religious celebration that occurred at the same time as the birth. Some of the less formal names for a baby girl were *Neferet*, "pretty one"; *Miut*, "kitty cat"; *Itesankh*, "Her father lives"; and *Aneksi*, "She belongs to me." A more formal female name would have been something like *Mutemwia*, which means "the goddess Mut is in her sacred boat." This would refer to the fact that the baby girl was born when the goddess Mut, the spouse of the god Amun of Karnak, had come out of her temple in a religious procession. Sometimes a formal name seems to reflect a problem with the birth or a concern that the child might not live, such as the name *Djedisetiusankh*, which translates into English as "Isis says that she shall live." A child was given only one name, and the name does not seem to have any connection to the name of the father or what we would call a family name. Nicknames were known, however, especially if someone had a particularly long name. The nickname was referred to as the "beautiful" or "good" name. For example, the princess Wattetkhethor had the beautiful name of Sesheshet, the "lotus."

There is written evidence of adoption in ancient Egypt, and adopting someone seems to have been a fairly simple process. It could be done if the couple did not have children, or if the man wanted a certain person to inherit from him, he could adopt that person. In the New Kingdom, adoption was also used to pass on an official position. Since a father always passed his job on to a family member, typically his oldest son, he could adopt someone if he wanted to pass his job on to them.

One adoption document from the reign of King Ramses XI (1099–1069) at the very end of the New Kingdom is quite interesting (Eyre 1992). A stable master named Nebnefer writes a document adopting his wife as his child, because they have no children, and he doesn't want anyone other than her to inherit from him. Seventeen years later, the wife, named Rennefer, writes a document saying that she and her husband had bought a female slave who had given birth to two girls and a boy, all of whom Rennefer had raised because she had no children of her own. Rennefer states that she gives these three children their freedom and also that her own brother, Padiu, has married one of the two girls. Rennefer then states that these four people, the three freed siblings and her brother, will inherit all her property. It would appear that Nebnefer was fairly well-off, and so it was important to make clear exactly who could inherit so as to protect their inheritance. This document is quite unusual, and it is not known how common it was for an ancient Egyptian man to have children from a woman who was not his wife in order to have an heir.

MOTHERHOOD

Numerous literary texts from ancient Egypt specifically mention the high regard in which mothers should be held. Women who had given birth and nurtured their children were seen as individuals who should be respected and cared for. In particular, sons seem to have been expected to love and honor their mothers and take care of them when they were old. The *Instructions of Any*, a didactic text composed in the early New Kingdom around 1500 BCE, admonishes a young man to support his mother with double the food she had given him, because "she had a heavy load in you, but she did not abandon you when you were born after your months. She was yet yoked, her breast in your mouth for three years" (Lichtheim 1976: 141).

In some ancient Egyptian literary teachings, which are referred to as "wisdom texts," women are portrayed as having two different natures: "good" and "bad." On the one hand, there is the perfect, virtuous wife and loving mother, and on the other hand, the strange, dangerous woman who can lead a man astray. All these "wisdom texts" contain advice for men about staying away from the second type of women and the consequences of not doing so. These texts seem to have been aimed at up-and-coming young officials and may have given this advice to protect their reputation, which was important for being promoted. This type of literature also stresses how important the ideal wife and mother was and how they were to be cherished and taken care of. Men were warned not to boss their wives around at home, not to start arguments with their wives, and when they have married and settled down, not to fool around with other women. There are documents that suggest it was a crime for a man to have sex with a married woman unless he was her husband. Along with the list of crimes committed by a corrupt foreman named Paneb at the village of Deir el-Medineh is the mention that he had sex with three women who were the wives of workmen. Included in the statements in the so-called Negative Confession of the Book of the Dead, which are recited in order to join Osiris and live in the afterlife, there is one that denies having had sex with a married woman.

An interesting will was written by an elderly woman and mother named Naunakhte, who lived in the New Kingdom village of Deir el-Medineh on the Theban West Bank (Černy 1945). She had first been married to a much older man, Qenherkhopshef, a scribe at the village, who died not long after and left her everything, as they did not seem to have had any children, although he may have had children from an earlier wife. (It makes one wonder if Qenherkhopshef had adopted Naunakhte in order to protect the inheritance that she would receive from him.) Naunakhte then remarries, a man named Khaemnun, a village workman, and they have eight children. In year 3 of the reign of Ramses V (about 1145 BCE), Naunakhte, who must be elderly by now, goes to the village court and writes a will in which she disinherits four of her eight children because they are not bothering to take care of her. She carefully states in the will that although they may inherit property that comes from their father, Khaemnun, they may not inherit any of her own property, which she had from her father and her first husband. A document written a year later acknowledges that Khaemnun came to the village court to request that Naunakhte's wishes be upheld and her property be handed out as she wished, so she must have passed away.

THE GODDESS ISIS AS THE PERFECT MOTHER

The role model for the perfect mother in ancient Egypt was the goddess Isis, who was important in the myth of Osiris. The earliest mention of this myth, and Isis as well, is in the Pyramid Texts, which first appeared in written form in pyramid burial chambers at the very end of the Fifth Dynasty (about 2375 BCE) of the Old Kingdom. Much later in the first century BCE, the Greek historian Plutarch wrote down the most complete version of the Osiris myth, and that is the one most people are familiar with today. Very briefly, the myth is as follows: Osiris was the husband-brother of Isis, and he ruled as the king of Egypt. Seth, the brother of Osiris, was jealous, as he wanted to be the king, and he killed Osiris. Isis and her sister, Nephthys, carefully protected and took care of the body of Osiris, such that he was able to impregnate Isis, even though he was dead. Isis hid away in the swamps of the delta when she was pregnant, so Seth could not find her. She continued to hide after giving birth to their son, Horus, and carefully guarded Horus until he was old enough to fight Seth. Horus avenged his father by defeating Seth and took the throne and ruled Egypt. Because of her sacrifice and care for both her husband and son, Isis was thought of as the goddess who embodied love and dedication to spouse and children.

Isis never had her own temple and cult until late in pharaonic times. The first temple dedicated entirely to her was on the island of Philae, at the south end of the First Cataract, the border with Nubia, built by King Amasis (570–526 BCE) of the Twenty-Sixth Dynasty. Hymns at the temple address her as "Lady of Heaven, Earth and the Netherworld," "who gave birth to all the gods," and "Divine Mother." Later in the Thirtieth Dynasty, King Nectanebo I (380–362 BCE) built a temple for Isis, referred to as the Iseum, at Behdet el-Hagar in the Egyptian delta. By the Ptolemaic Period, or the Greek time in Egypt, the cult of Isis as a universal goddess, perfect wife and mother, and a savior of people had spread throughout the ancient world.

ELDERLY WOMEN AND WIDOWS
IN ANCIENT EGYPT

Ancient Egyptian texts that discuss social behavior and good manners often mention that a well-brought-up man helps elderly people and takes care of widows. *The Instructions Addressed to King Merikare* date to the Eighteenth Dynasty (1550–1295 BCE) but are cast in the form of a First Intermediate Period (2160–2055 BCE) king giving advice to his son. In one section about being just, the king states, "Don't oppress the widow" (Lichtheim 1973: 100). In another text of this genre, *The Instruction of Amenemope*, which was written to outline behaviors for the ideal young man, the author says to leave a widow alone if you find her collecting grain left in the field after the harvest and be patient with her (Lichtheim 1976: 161). It may have been common, therefore, for widows who had been left without income to join in gleaning the grain fields to get grain for themselves. Rekhmire, the Theban vizier of King Thutmose III, states in his autobiography that "he protected the widow who did not have a husband" (see translation of primary text below). Just like what happens to women nowadays, ancient Egyptian women who lost husbands through divorce or death probably found themselves in economic difficulties. This is why having children was so important for women. An earlier autobiographical text in an Upper Egyptian tomb from the end of the Old Kingdom, or perhaps later, states that among the good deeds done by the tomb owner was "speaking up on behalf of the widow" (Strudwick 2005: 362), so possibly women on their own needed not only economic help but also help with legal or other issues.

Women with children who lived to adulthood certainly had a chance for a better life when they were elderly. The house census at Lahun shows that the soldier Hori had his mother living with him and his wife and son, and when he died, his son, Sneferu, kept both his mother and his grandmother in the house. In one of the letters from the landowner Heqanakht, he exhorts the person he sends it to: "[G]reet my mother Ipi a thousand times and a million times!" (Parkinson 1991: 105). Certainly, Ipi must have been a very respected member of the household. The elderly lady Naunakhte disinherits four of her children for not taking care of her now that she is old, but she has another four children who she says do take incredibly good care of her and to whom she wills her possessions.

Although the average life span in ancient Egypt was about thirty years, there were individuals who lived much longer. The main threat to a woman's life in ancient Egypt was childbirth, and if a woman lived through her childbearing years, she undoubtedly, like most women today, outlived men. Therefore, there would have been elderly widows in every community. There is not much evidence for elderly women in ancient Egyptian tomb scenes; as following the conventions of ancient Egyptian art, women were always to be shown young and beautiful. Minor or unimportant figures could be shown realistically, however, and from the Old Kingdom, there are scenes and statuettes of elderly women grinding grain and a few painted tomb scenes showing women with gray hair.

There is somewhat more evidence for elderly and widowed women in written documents and physical remains, especially from the New Kingdom workmen's village of Deir el-Medineh. A woman named Ii-Neferti was the wife of the workman Sennedjem. Their family tomb in the cemetery west of the village was discovered and opened in 1886 and contained the bodies of twenty people. The coffin and objects of Ii-Neferti were sent to the Metropolitan Museum in New York. Eventually her mummy was unwrapped and sent to the Peabody Museum in Cambridge, Massachusetts. A study of the body in 1933 concluded that based on cranial sutures, tooth loss, and arthritis, the skeleton suggested an advanced age of seventy-five years. Although it would be good to have a more modern study done to verify Ii-Neferti's age, clearly her skeleton is one of an older woman.

A stela belonging to Ii-Neferti was removed from one of the chapels at Deir el-Medineh in 1818 and is now in the Bankes Collection in Dorset, England. It shows her kneeling and adoring the moon god Thoth and begging him for forgiveness, because he had caused her to see "darkness by day." This is possibly the ancient Egyptian phrase for blindness, although some scholars interpret it as describing depression. Standing behind her and also adoring the god is her grandson Anhotep. Ii-Neferti asking for forgiveness was the focus and reason for the carving of the stela, so she is the largest figure on it. Her husband, Sennedjem, does not appear with her, as by the conventions of ancient Egyptian art, he then would have been the focus of the stela and be the largest figure. We don't know when Ii-Neferti or her husband died, and whether or not she was a widow in her old age, but statistically speaking, she probably was.

DOCUMENT: VIZER REKHMIRE, THEBAN TOMB 100

These lines were part of the autobiographical text of the Eighteenth Dynasty Vizer Rekhmire, who served King Thutmose III (1425–1479 BCE). The tomb is Theban Tomb 100 on the West Bank of the Nile at Thebes, modern Luxor. The text is on the wall of the south end of the transverse hall inside his tomb.

I defended the widow who did not have a husband. I established the son and heir upon the seat of his father. I gave bread to the hungry, water to the thirsty, and meat, ointment and clothing to him who had none.

Source: Sethe, Kurt. *Urkunden der 18. Dynastie*. Berlin: Akademie-Verlag, 1961, p. 1078, lines 6–10. Translated by Lisa Sabbahy from the hieroglyphic text.

2

WORK, ECONOMY, AND LAW

"Now what am I supposed to do?" Irer thought to herself. She had just finished her monthly rotation as wab-priestess in the temple of the deceased king, Senusret II, at Lahun. She always left her time in the temple humbled but content. . . . She had served the eternal soul of the king. Now, as overseer of weaving, she has to get a letter sent off to that useless official in charge of paying the weavers. He never showed up with their rations, so they stopped weaving. The slave women cannot weave, so nothing can be done. The warp threads are on the looms with no one to weave! I must get to the scribe and have a letter done. I must remember to tell the scribe to refer to him as lord, and say "may you live, prosper and be happy," and also say several times in the letter that I am his humble servant; then maybe he will take note and send food provisions so that the weavers go back to work.

UNDERSTANDING THE POSITION AND ROLE OF WOMEN IN ANCIENT EGYPT

A large amount of both written and pictorial evidence exists to tell us about women in ancient Egypt. We can glimpse into the lives of royal females, noble women, as well as peasant women, but it is questionable how accurately we understand their actual status and role in ancient Egyptian society. Most of the pictorial evidence preserved is from tombs, which only royalty or nobility could afford, and the relief scenes and statuary in the tombs depict a perfect world meant for the eternal afterlife and are not a truly realistic depiction of everyday life. Royal women had their own tombs, but nonroyal women shared the tomb of their husband, in which the husband was the central figure, and women were shown according to an elite male perspective, which was produced by artists and craftsmen who were all male.

Elite women, depicted in statuary or scenes in their husbands' tombs, are represented following the gendered conventions of ancient Egyptian art. The woman is shown light-skinned, reflecting the fact that she spends her time indoors rather than out in the sun. She is also shown in passive poses and in statuary stands with both feet together, unmoving, whereas men are always shown striding and therefore busy. One Egyptologist even wrote an article entitled "Did Women 'Do Things' in Ancient Egypt" (Routledge 2008) because of the way women are always portrayed as passive, compared to men. A common scene in elite tombs is the man fishing and fowling in the marshes. The man stands in a striding position in the papyrus skiff, spearing fish and taking down birds with a throw stick. His wife is usually much smaller and sitting down, often clinging to his leg. Sometimes she points out prey to him. His daughters can also be in the skiff, and they are in the same poses as their mother. Routledge goes on to discuss the ancient Egypt phrase meaning "to do something" and points out that it was never applied to female action in ancient Egypt, except once for Queen Hatshepsut when she was king.

That a woman is shown physically smaller than her husband, and is also shown touching or embracing him, and not the other way around, stresses her secondary or inferior position to her husband. In ancient Egyptian art, the person touching someone else is considered to be less important than the person being touched. There is a statue of General Horemheb, before he was king, from his nonroyal tomb at Saqqara. He sits next to his wife, and instead of her reaching over to embrace him, he reaches over to her and holds her hand. Horemheb must have requested that their statues be carved in such a way, clearly reflecting his affection for his wife.

Another characteristic for showing the dominant or most important individual in ancient Egyptian art is expressed by who is on the left side, from the point of view of the person facing the piece of art. In statues portraying the tomb owner and his wife, almost without exception, the tomb owner is on the left and his wife on the right. The same position can be seen on stelae, as well, with the deceased on the left and his children offering to him, standing on the right. If a stela showed the king offering to a god, the god would be on the left and the king on the right and so on.

Art in ancient Egypt, in terms of statuary and painted scenes, was associated with a tomb or temple and had a religious purpose. All statuary that would have been carved in stone or wood, for women, would have depicted them standing or seated, alone or with a husband or children, and would have been placed in the serdab of the tomb in which she was buried. In this small, enclosed chamber, referred to as a *serdab*, the *ka*, or soul, of the woman could manifest and take part in receiving the offerings of food and drink brought to the tomb by the *ka*-priestess or priest. The tomb scenes in which women appeared would have shown them sitting by themselves or, more likely, with their husband; being offered food and drink; or watching scenes of daily life in their estate, where their edible offerings would be produced.

In a tomb scene or statue, an elite woman was depicted only young and beautiful, the perfect state that she should be in forever. On the other hand, non-elite women could be represented in daily life scenes in tombs, taking part in the activities of the tomb owner's estate. In these scenes, non-elite women would be active and working: weaving, mixing mash for beer, grinding grain, serving food, and pulling up flax. Their figures are not bound by the same conventions as elite women, because what is important to show is the production of food and goods for the afterlife and not the people doing it. For this reason, non-elite women can also be shown old, wrinkled, and bent over.

Representations of women in written evidence are more balanced, in the sense that we have letters and documents from people in everyday life and situations, but again the people doing the writing always appear to have been male. Although scholars assume that there were "pockets" of female literacy among the royalty and nobility, there is no direct proof for female literacy in ancient Egypt. We can reconstruct a view of the lives of women in ancient Egypt, but it is filtered through a masculine lens, as it is both described and depicted for us only by men.

WOMEN AT WORK

"A woman is asked about her husband. A man is asked about his rank" (Lichtheim 1976: 140). This saying comes from *The*

Instructions of Any, a text to explain to up-and-coming young officials how to behave. It was composed in the Eighteenth Dynasty (1550–1295 BCE). The statement given is very reminiscent of conversations at modern cocktail parties, where people ask women, "And what does your husband do?"

Ancient Egyptian women held many different types of jobs, and these jobs changed, sometimes quite dramatically, throughout the long span of almost three thousand years of pharaonic civilization. One thing that did not change, however, was that women in ancient Egypt never held government positions. They never had jobs in the administration of the country. From the king on down, the power structure of ancient Egypt was entirely male. This is rather odd, as for the most part, in all other aspects of life, men and women in ancient Egypt were fairly equal, but women never served as government officials.

This situation must be related in some way to the fact that women were not sent to school and trained as scribes. Certainly, there must have been "pockets" of literate women in elite and royal families. For example, there seems to be enough indirect evidence to assume that some women at the workmen's village at Deir el-Medineh could read and write. But everything preserved about school in ancient Egypt is about schoolboys and male tutors and teachers. In the context of education and school, females are never mentioned. In order to be a government official, one had to be literate, or be a scribe, as reading and writing documents were essential for the functioning of governmental bureaucracy. Even though the vast majority of the ancient Egyptian population was illiterate, their country functioned very bureaucratically with endless numbers of documents. That so many of these documents have been preserved has made possible that we fairly accurately understand many aspects of life in ancient Egypt.

Evidence for the different jobs that were held by women comes either from inscriptions giving the name of a woman with a title that reflects her job or from a tomb scene that actually shows a woman at work. For the most part, non-elite women are the ones represented in the daily life scenes in tombs, showing the activities going on at the tomb owner's estate. These scenes focus on agriculture and the production of food that was offered on a daily basis to the soul of the deceased.

It was also non-elite women who made up the largest portion of the female population in ancient Egypt. These working women are shown in such activities as spinning and weaving, sieving the mash for beer, grinding the grain for bread, and serving food. Women did not do agricultural labor, other than winnowing grain after it had been threshed or pulling up the stalks of flax that would be used to make linen thread for weaving. In tomb scenes that are associated with the tomb owner's funeral or funerary cult, non-elite women are shown as professional mourners. Two women play the parts of the two goddesses Isis and Nephthys, protecting the coffin at the head and the foot, while other women in the procession wailed, wept, and threw dust over themselves.

Women as professional musicians and singers were most common in the New Kingdom (1550–1069 BCE). They are depicted in tomb scenes entertaining guests at a festival, such as the Beautiful Festival of the Valley that was held on the West Bank of Thebes. While the image of the god Amun was carried in procession to each of the royal mortuary temples on the West Bank, families celebrated by holding feasts in the courtyards of, or nearby, their tombs. The musicians worked in groups of three, with one woman playing the harp, another the lute, and the third with a double flute, lyre, or a tambourine. Singers also were usually in a group of three. The ancient Egyptians used the number three to express the plural, so showing three singers might actually mean that there were lots of them. There could also be women who sat and clapped with their hands, to keep time. There were sometimes a few dancers with the musicians, or some of the musicians were quite animated, moving as they played.

Often the only dancers portrayed are those in a religious context, particularly in rituals or festivals for, or associated with, the goddess Hathor. Hathor's dancers were in a group known as the *khener*. These women were often tattooed, and the dances were quite acrobatic. They are depicted dancing with clappers and also mirrors, and other women standing by them shake the musical instruments symbolic of the Hathoric cult, the *menat* necklace and the *sistrum*. The members of the *khener* often used to sing as well.

The *khener* dancers actually can be found in a range of contexts using dance. There were *khener* dancers for the king's court. There were *khener* dancers for the temples of a number of gods and goddesses other than Hathor. There were also *khener* dancers for women giving birth, and some scholars think that these dancers were also midwives. In ancient Egyptian thought, rebirth after death was parallel to childbirth, so having the *khener* dancers at a childbirth, as well as at a funeral, was logical.

WOMEN'S WORK IN THE OLD KINGDOM

In terms of titles, from the period of the Old Kingdom (2650–2150 BCE), women held titles such as weaver, overseer of weavers, singer, overseer of singers, dancer, grinder of grains, food vendor, winnower, domestic servant, hairdresser, stewardess of the queen's household, as well as overseer of ornaments, overseer of cloth, and seal bearer. Women of elite status, because of their husbands' position as important officials, could be part of the royal court and, therefore, carry a title such as "noblewoman of the king," or "ornament of the king," although titles such as these probably reflected the woman's status and not an actual job. "Ornament of the king" was also a title held by many priestesses of Hathor.

Women could hold religious positions that gave them a title of priestess. A *ka*-priestess, a woman who maintained tomb offerings, offered food at the tomb of a deceased person on a daily basis. The ancient Egyptians believed that the dead had the same everyday needs as the living, and so the deceased had to be fed and taken care of. The food came from a farm or "estate" owned by the family of the deceased and was supplied to the *ka*-priestess. The food offered to the dead was thought only to be partaken of by the soul of the deceased, and therefore, the food was taken home by the priestess, and that was her pay. A woman could become a *ka*-priestess by being asked to serve as one by the tomb owner before they died or by inheriting the job from someone in her family. Often it seems that women carried out this job in the place of their husbands. It could be that the husband had died and this was a way widows could keep an income. A position of *ka*-priest was typical for men, and in fact, there were many more *ka*-priests than *ka*-priestesses.

PRIESTESSES OF HATHOR AND NEITH

Also in the Old Kingdom, many women, both elite and non-elite, and also princesses, were priestesses of the goddess Hathor or the goddess Neith. There were over four hundred Hathor priestesses during this time, and there were temples or chapels for Hathor throughout Egypt. Some women, although not as many, were also priestesses of Neith, whose cult was not as widespread as that of Hathor. Not much is known about the goddess Neith, although her importance goes back to the beginning of ancient Egyptian history. She was a protective goddess and, early on, was associated with hunting and warfare. She is depicted as a woman in a long dress, wearing the Red Crown on her head. The Red Crown is associated with the delta, or Lower Egypt, and in the Late Period (664–30 BCE), the cult center of Neith was at the city of Sais in the delta.

Hathor, on the other hand, was the most important female related to Ra, the god of the sun who created the world and everything in it. Hathor was Ra's wife, and therefore the mother of the king, as the sun god was the king's father. In some myths, Hathor was the daughter of the sun god as well, as Hathor functioned as the "feminine element" anytime the sun god needed one. Hathor was depicted as a woman with horns and a sun disk on her head. She could also appear in animal form as a cow. Hathor is tied to women and childbirth, as well as dance, drinking, and music. The main temple of Hathor was located at Dendera in Upper Egypt, just south of Abydos.

The priestesses of Hathor held two objects that were associated with the goddess. The first was a *menat*, a necklace of very heavy beads attached to a counterpoise. The second object was a *sistrum*, a rattling instrument held by a handle and shaken. Hathor priestesses in the Old Kingdom often wore a red scarf around their neck, letting it fall down their back, when taking part in rituals and offerings to the goddess. These priestesses took care of the offerings and rituals in the temples, where they were also joined by other women who were singers, musicians, and dancers. A special group of dancers called the *khener* was known from the time of the Fifth Dynasty (2494–2345 BCE) onward. They were most commonly known as dancers for the goddess Hathor, and their dance group could include men as well. They held clappers in the shape of hands, as well as mirrors, which probably symbolized the sun disk, while they danced. Representing the goddess Hathor, the *khener* danced at funerary feasts as well as at childbirth celebrations. Rebirth and birth were both associated with Hathor, as she was the mythical mother of the newborn sun god.

WOMEN'S WORK IN THE MIDDLE KINGDOM

By the beginning of the Middle Kingdom (1970–1640 BCE), women's titles had undergone quite a change. Titles such as "overseer" or "inspector," or titles indicating work or status of importance in the royal palace, were no longer held by women, with the only exception being the title "overseer of weavers." Middle

Kingdom women no longer appear to have had any positions of authority over others, even in household labor. Another noticeable difference between the Old and Middle Kingdoms was that work in the Middle Kingdom seems to be much more clearly differentiated between males and females. With very few exceptions, titles show that women worked inside buildings, while men did any kind of work that was outside or away from the home. Men did all agricultural labor as well as crafts. It was only in the production of textiles, which were produced inside a house or workshop, that women, not men, were the important laborers and did the spinning and weaving. Men are really not weavers until the New Kingdom (1550–1069 BCE), when the vertical loom is introduced and used instead of the horizontal one. A vertical, or upright, loom needs more shoulder strength, and that is thought to be the reason that men started weaving.

THE IMPORTANCE OF TEXTILES AND WEAVING

Textiles were used extensively in ancient Egypt for both the living and the dead. People needed clothing and bedding, and the dead needed to be wrapped. Textiles are already known in Neolithic times, around 5000 BCE from the area of the Fayum, and were produced by people referred to by archaeologists as the Fayum A culture, probably the earliest people known in Egypt to have settled down and domesticated both plants and animals. The majority of all the textiles in Egypt are linen, which is made from the fibers of the flax plant. Pieces of linen textiles were found in the Fayum when excavations in the 1920s discovered the Fayum A remains. The fibers from the flax plant first have to be spun to produce thread, which was then wound into coils or balls. This process needed spinning whorls, made in stone, and spinning bowls that were mostly pottery but could also be stone. Because stone preserves so well, finding spinning whorls at an ancient site serves as evidence that thread was being spun and textiles must have been woven. Ancient Egyptian women wove on horizontal wooden looms until the New Kingdom when vertical looms were used. Since wood is perishable, the only archaeological evidence for a loom would be the post holes left in the ground from the four pegs at the corners of the loom. Vertical looms needed to be steadied at the top, so they were set up against a wall. If it was set against a stone wall, holes were cut for the loom pegs, and these holes can still be identified.

A finely woven linen sheet from the storehouses of Queen Hatshepsut of the Eighteenth Dynasty. (The Metropolitan Museum of Art)

By the time of the Middle Kingdom (2055–1650 BCE), there are tomb scenes, especially at Beni Hassan in northern Upper Egypt, that show women working in all the stages of producing thread from flax fibers and weaving it into linen cloth. Stalks of flax are pulled out of the ground and then broken open with sticks to remove the fibers. The fibers are then spliced together to form one long thread and wrapped into balls of thread. To make sure that the thread is strong enough, two single threads were spun together. This part of the process needed spindles and spinning bowls. Simultaneously, two threads are fed through spinning bowls to moisten them, and then they are pulled up to a spindle on which they are spun. The women stand, pull the threads together onto the spindle, roll the spindle on their thigh to roll up the threads, and drop the spindle to pull and extend the thread. This process would have taken many days to create enough thread to weave a useable piece of cloth. The thread was then wrapped around pegs on the wall to be ready for weaving. These scenes at Beni Hassan also include a woman who is clearly older than the women spinning and weaving, and above her is written the title "overseer of the weaving."

THE CHANGE OF WOMEN'S TITLES
WITH THE MIDDLE KINGDOM

It would appear that in the time called the First Intermediate Period (2160–2055 BCE), which came between the Old and Middle Kingdoms, there were political and social changes that brought about women being more closely tied to house and family, while men became more dominant in anything that was outside of the household and was of economic importance. This situation came about because of two changes: one having to do with the climate and the other one political. By the end of the Old Kingdom, the Egyptian climate had become very dry. Rainfall had stopped, and the grasslands on each side of the Nile River had become the deserts that one sees in Egypt today. This change happened along with a period of erratic Niles that caused low inundations and famine. There is evidence from the autobiographies inscribed in the tombs of high officials in provincial towns that there was not enough water in the river, crops could not be grown, and local people had to be supplied with rations of food to keep them from starving.

Also, at the end of the Old Kingdom, central control of the country from the capital at Memphis was lost, and civil war between the nomes, or provinces, broke out. The situation may simply have been too dangerous, so women chose to stay at or near home to protect themselves and their children. There is no clear evidence that this is what happened, but the status of women changed dramatically, and scholars have never really addressed that change. Finally, King Mentuhotep II (2055–2004 BCE), who came from Thebes, defeated the line of kings at Heracleopolis who had taken over from the kings at Memphis and reunited Egypt, beginning the period called the Middle Kingdom.

One important new female title, *nebet per*, "mistress of the house," appeared with the beginning of the Middle Kingdom, around 2055 BCE, and became the most important female title of that period. Scholars assume that the title *nebet per* indicated a married woman and was the equivalent of the modern title "housewife." This new title seems to go hand in hand with the fact that women at this time were closely tied to work that was inside their house. Another change at this time was the disappearance, for the most part, of the title "priestess." When the Middle Kingdom began, only a few women still held the title of "priestess," and they were all wives of very high officials, particularly nomarchs, who ruled over provinces in ancient Egypt. Earlier, in the Old Kingdom, more than four hundred women had held the title "priestess," and these women came from all levels of society and had served at temples of Hathor in the area near Memphis, or in Upper Egypt. By the later part of the Middle Kingdom, the title of priestess of Hathor disappeared completely. The religious cults of Hathor continued to be taken care of because the male title "priest" never disappeared.

WOMEN'S TITLES IN THE NEW KINGDOM

When the title of priestess disappeared, wives of high officials took on the religious title *shemayit*, or "chantress" of a deity, particularly of the god Amun, whose religious center was at Karnak Temple at Thebes. There were also some chantresses of the goddess Hathor. "Chantress" seems to be the only nonroyal female religious title that existed in the New Kingdom (1550–1069 BCE). Some scholars see the title "chantress" as a position equivalent to that of priestess but with different duties. A chantress accompanied priests in the temple providing calming hymns and prayers to please the god or goddess. The chantress held the rattling instrument called a *sistrum* as well as a heavy bead necklace, called a *menat*, that was attached to a counterpoise. Both the *sistrum* and the *menat* were objects sacred to the goddess Hathor, and they were shaken to create a noise considered soothing to the goddess. The noise they made was supposed to mimic the sound Hathor made as a cow when she walked through rustling papyrus plants. In the beginning, the chantresses of the New Kingdom were always wives of upper-middle-class or elite officials, and these women all had the same two main titles: "mistress of the house" and "chantress of Amun."

Another title of importance that could be held by wives of high officials in the New Kingdom was *menat nesut*, "wet nurse of the king." This woman would have been virtually part of the royal family, and her position would have meant not only royal favor for her but perhaps also advancement for male members of her family. Two of the better known royal wet nurses were Sitra, the nurse of Queen Hatshepsut, and Maia, the nurse of Tutankhamun. A rather damaged sandstone statue (JE 56264) in the Egyptian Museum in Cairo depicted Sitra seated with the small child Hatshepsut, mostly broken away, on her lap (Roehrig 1996: 17). When the statue was carved, Hatshepsut was already king, but she is depicted in the statue as a child king. What is left of her figure shows her wearing the *shedjet*-kilt, the royal kilt, and her sandals rest on a depiction of the Nine Bows, representing the enemies of Egypt. Only the king stands on the Nine Bows. Sitra must have been very important to Hatshepsut, because she seems to have been buried in tomb KV 60 in the Valley of the Kings.

A carved wall scene in the tomb of Maia, the wet nurse of Tutankhamun, discovered in North Saqqara in 1996, still preserves the figure of Maia, along with Tutankhamun, as a little boy, seated on her lap facing her (Zivie 2007: 73). Tutankhamun wears the Blue Crown of the king, and his name in the tomb is Tutankhamun, not Tutankhaten, which means the royal court had already left the city of Amarna, moving back to the capital at Memphis, when this tomb was decorated.

THE VILLAGE MARKET

In Old Kingdom, tombs at Saqqara are scenes of marketplaces with women busily selling and trading. As there was not yet currency in ancient Egyptian times, things were either traded or sold in exchange for a certain amount of grain or copper, or the value of things as calculated on how much grain or copper it would be worth. For the most part, women are seen selling fruits, vegetables, and textiles, as well as selling beer to drink. In one of the Fifth Dynasty (2494–2345 BCE) tombs, above a woman pouring beer into a pottery bowl, it says in hieroglyphs "bowl woman," and the man drinking the beer says that "the grain is good." In the New Kingdom, there are scenes in Eighteenth Dynasty (1550–1295 BCE) tombs at Thebes depicting women selling things in marketplaces that are clearly alongside the river. The people buying their goods are men getting off the boats that tie up at a nearby harbor. The women are selling goods that they make at home anyway, such as loaves of bread, beer, or woven linen cloth, and taking them to the marketplace to sell and help out with their household expenses. In this way, their work is still traditional as it is tied to something they do at home.

WOMEN AND LAW

Upholding "justice" or "truth" was very important in ancient Egypt. The concept of truth was personified as a goddess named Maat, who had existed at the time when the world was created. The most important responsibility of an ancient Egyptian king was to uphold Maat and therefore uphold world order and defeat chaos.

This kept the gods and goddesses happy and all of Egypt as well. The vizier, who was the most powerful official under the king, had many responsibilities, including being the chief justice of Egypt. As such, the vizier held the title of "High Priest of Maat," who had to see that law, known as *hep* in ancient Egypt, was upheld.

When a court case had to be heard, a group of judges was put together. If it were a serious case, it would have been heard in one of the Great Courts, which seem to have been in Memphis and Thebes. The vizier would pick from important officials, such as high priests, army officials, or mayors of towns to judge the case. Otherwise, the case could be heard in a local court, known as a *kenbet*. The defendant would explain their case, and the judges, perhaps after questioning witnesses, would hand down a decision. There were no lawyers or jury. If it were a criminal case, the defendant or defendants would be "questioned by the stick." A defendant could also be asked to take an oath, called the "Great Oath," which invokes both the god and the king, and it seems that lying under oath could bring the death penalty.

From what we can tell, women in ancient Egypt enjoyed legal equality with men. Women could inherit property and will it as they pleased. They could buy, sell, and trade, although a man often handled business and property for his wife. Women could bring cases in court and also serve as witnesses. They could also be arrested, tried, and given similar punishments to those of men. If women were divorced, they retained their personal property and received one-third of the communal property. If the woman was being divorced because of committing adultery, she lost her third of the communal property. In the Late Period (664–332 BCE), a woman could have a "marriage contract" stating that her husband had to pay her a specified sum in order to divorce her. These contracts seem to have originated to keep men from divorcing their wives to marry other, and usually younger, women.

HERYA, THE CRIMINAL

The trial of a lady named Herya was written on an ostracon, a fragment of limestone, used to write on, and was discovered at the workmen's village of Deir el-Medineh on the West Bank of Thebes. It is dated to the sixth year of the king Seti II (about 1194 BCE). A workman named Nebnefer went to the village court, or *kenbet*, and said that a copper chisel that he had in his house was gone. This chisel was undoubtedly government property, because the workmen in the village were given their tools and equipment by the government. Nebnefer had asked everyone in the village, but no one knew anything about it. Then a woman came to him and said that she had a dream, a "divine manifestation," and in it she saw that Herya took the chisel.

Herya was brought to the court, but she denied that she took the chisel. Herya took an oath in the name of Amun and the king, stating that she had not taken it. The court sent one of the village men back to Herya's house with her to search her house, and he came back with the chisel and also objects that had been stolen from the village temple of Amun. There is no mention of Herya's husband or children being present in the court case. It would be odd if Herya had a house in the village without a husband who was a workman, as the village belonged to the government, who gave houses to each of the workmen, but no husband is mentioned.

Finding these objects meant that Herya was guilty not only of theft but of perjury as well. Stealing the chisel belonging to the government and stealing the objects from the temple were both crimes against the state, as was taking a false oath in the name of Amun and the king, and so Herya faced the death penalty. The verdict of the court stated, "Mrs. Herya is a great criminal who deserves death. The workman Nebnefer is in the right" (Donker van Heel 2016: 57). The local judges had their decision taken to the vizier, and the vizier ordered Herya taken to the river bank. Being taken to the river bank has been interpreted in different ways. Some scholars assume that she was going to be put to death by drowning. Others have wondered if she would be fed to crocodiles. Or, was Herya to be executed in some other way, and her body thrown into the river, so that she would not be allowed a proper burial? Egyptologists still don't know the meaning of this statement. There is not much evidence about how the death penalty was carried out, except that in Ramesside times (1265–1069 BCE), which is when Herya lived, tomb robbers were sentenced to death by being impaled on a sharp stick.

CRIME AND PUNISHMENT

Punishment for crimes in ancient Egypt was mostly physical and was carried out right after the verdict was decided. For example, if a person was found guilty of stealing something from someone else, they would be beaten and forced to return what had been stolen, as well as possibly having to pay a certain amount to the person they stole from. People were not given jail sentences like nowadays, although they could be sent to the equivalent of an agricultural labor camp or to a quarry and made to do hard labor. Women were not exempt from being forced to do hard labor. For example, in the time of King Thutmose III, if a man ran away to avoid military service, his entire family could be sent to labor in a quarry as punishment.

The standard punishment handed out for a serious crime was one hundred blows and five pierced wounds, although it is not clear what part of the body was pierced and how it was done. If the crime was serious enough, people could also be punished with having their ears and nose cut off. A papyrus known as the Judicial Papyrus of Turin, as it is in the Turin Museum in Italy, records the trial and punishment of more than thirty people who were associated in various ways with the assassination of King Ramses III (1184–1153 BCE) in the Twentieth Dynasty. Different types of punishments were given out, depending on the extent of the person's involvement in the assassination conspiracy. The document gives five different lists of people based on their punishments, going from most severe to least severe. In the first list were seventeen men and six women, who were wives of some of them. They were sentenced to death, but the way in which they were to die was not written in the document. It is also interesting that the six women were just listed as "six women" and their names were not given, although all the men were named.

The next list was of people left unnamed, and one who was named, who colluded with the conspirators and were also sentenced to death. However, this time it is stated that they were not harmed and took their own lives. The next group of people listed included the prince, Pentawere, who was set to seize the throne when his father was killed. The document states that all these people committed suicide. There is no evidence how this was done, however. The next list was of people who were punished by having their nose and ears cut off and mentioned that one of these men then committed suicide. At the very end of the document, a man was listed as having been scolded but left alone.

The main person in the conspiracy to kill the king was one of the king's three wives, Tiye, who wanted her oldest son, Pentawere, to take the throne. Apparently, the conspiracy started with her and women allied with her in the harem. The king had another queen, Isis Ta-Hemdjert, and a third queen, also with the name Tiye, who seems to have been the most important of the queens, as she held the title of the "King's Great Wife," and as such, her oldest son should take the throne. Indeed, it was her son, Ramses IV, who took over the throne upon the death of his father.

The minor queen Tiye and the ladies of the harem are mentioned in the Judicial Papyrus, as the people found guilty conspired with them, but the punishment for the queen and her harem ladies is never mentioned. Her son is clearly stated to have been left to commit suicide, but nothing is said about the queen. It is possible that part of the document is missing, as it was cut into pieces when it was found in the 1800s. It might also have been considered inappropriate to record the punishment of a royal wife.

SOLVING LEGAL MATTERS WITH THE ORACLE

An oracle of the deified king Amenhotep I was used in the Nineteenth and Twentieth Dynasties (1295–1069 BCE) at Deir el-Medineh to settle disputes between the villagers. The oracle seemed to be equal to having a dispute heard in the local court and perhaps, because what the oracle said was divine, carried more weight. On festival days, workmen of the village who acted as the priests for the cult of King Amenhotep I and his mother Ahmose-Nefertari came out of their chapel carrying a statue of Amenhotep I. The village of Deir el-Medineh was supposed to have been founded in the time of Amenhotep I, and he and his mother were considered to be the patron saints of the village.

The statue of Amenhotep I would have been in a wooden litter on two poles, with four priests holding up each pole on their shoulders. The movement of the priests carrying the statue determined the answers to the questions asked. If the answer was a "yes," the priests would carry the statue forward, while if the answer was "no," they would move backward. Sometimes two ostraca, which were small pieces of pottery or limestone, were written on with two different answers and buried on opposite sides of the path that the oracle procession would follow. If the priests carrying the image dipped in one direction or the other, then the answer was given. The oracle might also be asked who in the village stole a particular object. Then priests would carry the king's image throughout the village until it stopped at the door of the guilty person. Both men and women could consult the oracle. Questions asked by men seem to have been tied to their work and wages, while questions from women dealt more with disputes about personal property.

Oracles had been used earlier in the Eighteenth Dynasty to show divine approval for royal decisions. One interesting use of the oracle was by Queen Hatshepsut. She was the regent for her stepson-nephew Thutmose III when he became king because he was too young to rule on his own. Then, instead of staying regent, she had herself proclaimed king along with him, in a situation called a co-regency. Usually a co-regency came about when a father proclaimed his son king with him, so in case he died, the son was already ruling. Hatshepsut, however, went from queen regent to king. She was very cognizant of the fact that her rule as king might be questioned, and so she issued a great deal of propaganda about the fact that the god Amun was her divine father and that he wanted her to rule. Hatshepsut stressed that she carried out Amun's every command and everything she did was for him.

In year nine of her joint reign with Thutmose III, Hatshepsut decided to send an expedition to the land of Punt, which was along the coast of the southern part of the Red Sea. Punt could have been in the area of Eretria, or possibly Somalia, or even Saudi Arabia on the other side of the Red Sea. The ancient Egyptians had gone to Punt for myrrh and frankincense in the Old and Middle Kingdoms in order to use it in temple rituals. Hatshepsut used an oracle to show that the god Amun commanded her to go to Punt and get myrrh for his temple rituals. This oracle was not one in which the priests moved the figure of the god in order to answer; this oracle actually had a voice that came from the stand on which the god's divine boat carrying his statue was placed. Hatshepsut says in her inscription about the oracle that she actually heard a command from the god himself.

DOCUMENT: QUEEN HATSHEPSUT, MORTUARY TEMPLE AT DEIR EL-BAHARI

The following text is from the back wall of the first portico of the mortuary temple of Queen Hatshepsut at Deir el-Bahari on the West Bank of Thebes. She is explaining that in an oracle at Karnak Temple, she asked what to do for her father the god Amun. He commanded her to go to Punt and get myrrh, and she did exactly what he commanded. Notice that the masculine pronoun "he" is used, even for Hatshepsut, as the king of Egypt should be male.

"The Majesty of the palace, may he live, prosper and be healthy, appealed at the steps of the throne of the lord of the gods.

A command was heard from the great throne, an oracle of the god himself: Search out the ways to Punt! Explore the ways to the hillsides of myrrh!"

In response Hatshepsut answered:

"I will lead the army on water and on land to bring the marvels of Punt to this god."

Source: Sethe, Kurt. *Urkunden der 18. Dynastie* IV. Berlin: Akademie-Verlag, 1961, p. 342, lines 10–17. Translated by Lisa Sabbahy from the hieroglyphic text.

3

LITERACY, EDUCATION, AND HEALTH

Henut was so excited. Today was school day, and several boys from their neighborhood would join her brother for lessons with their father, and so would she! Her father was a "Scribe of the Granary" and had been away lately, but now that he was back, lessons would start again. She had practiced and practiced writing letters to officials just like their father had taught them. Over and over again, wetting her rush pen and scrapping on her black-powdered disk to get ink, she carefully wrote on her whitewashed wooden board: "This is a communication to the lord, life, prosperity and health, that all the affairs of the lord, life, prosperity and health, are safe and sound in their places . . ." Her mother said she was getting too much black ink on her linen tunics and the washerman was complaining, but she said it with a twinkle in her eye.

WHO WAS LITERATE IN ANCIENT EGYPT?

Ancient civilizations did not have high rates of literacy. A majority of people had to spend their time working, or their families would have nothing to eat. Learning to read and write took time that most people could not afford to give up, along with the fact that a person did not need to be literate to raise animals or grow plants, which is what most ancient Egyptian peasants did. It is a guess, but an educated one, that in the Old Kingdom (2686–2160 BCE), probably 1% of the population was literate, but by the later New Kingdom (1295–1069 BCE), there is clearly more literacy, and perhaps 5% of the population was literate. The majority of these literate people would have been male officials working in government administration. Literacy in ancient Egypt can be thought of as a very high-status skill as it was demanded of any man who wanted to work his way up through the administration of the government, the army, or the priesthood. For women, who did not have careers in any of these administrative branches, literacy was not necessary but undoubtedly was attained by a small number of women, particularly in elite and royal families where women would have been property owners and controlled a fair amount of wealth.

WHAT WAS EDUCATION LIKE IN ANCIENT EGYPT?

For the vast majority of ancient Egyptians, education consisted of what they learned from their fathers and mothers. Most boys would have learned how to farm from working with their fathers, and those who were sons of craftsmen learned those skills from their fathers. Mothers would have taught their daughters all they needed to know to run a household and cook, deal with common illnesses, as well as possibly weaving and sewing. What we would call "school" education was limited to elite and royal boys. Schools were located in the royal residence, sometimes in temples, as well as in the households of scribes who gave lessons. Our information about these schools comes from autobiographies and texts that school boys copied. Schooling seems to have started around the age of five or six and lasted four years. Then a boy would work as a trainee in either a branch of the government or the army or join the priesthood.

The material learned at school was writing and reading hieratic, which is cursive handwriting, along with arithmetic. Arithmetic consisted of working with fractions and working out basic geometry problems, such as finding the area of a triangle or the volume of a cylinder. Handwriting was done in ligatures, or small groups of signs connected together. Many of the hieratic texts given to the students to read and copy consisted of reasons why a young man would want to be a scribe and descriptions of how lucky one was to be a scribe. Papyrus Lansing, dating to the later New Kingdom (1186–1069 BCE), contains lines such as "Writing for him who knows it is better than all other professions"; "Be a scribe! Your body will be sleek; your hand will be soft"; and "You call for one, a thousand answer you; You stride freely on the road." There are also texts that warn about not being a bad student. One part has the teacher telling a student that "[y]our heart is denser than a great obelisk." The ancient Egyptians thought that what we know goes on in the brain went on in the heart, so this is equivalent to telling the student that he is a blockhead. The teacher goes on to say, "[T]hough I beat you with every type of stick, you do not listen" (Lichtheim 1976: 168–71).

At school, beginning scribes wrote on small wooden boards coated with whitewash; it could be easily cleaned off with something wet and reused. They wrote with a rush pen in black ink made from charcoal. The pen tip was dipped in water and then scrapped across a hard disk of powdered charcoal. The teacher corrected in red ink, which, of course, still happens today. Scribes carried a thin rectangular wooden palette with them, which had at the top two round inkwells for black- and red-powdered disks and a cavity the middle to keep pens. Scribes also had to carry with them a small jar or pot with water to wet the rush pens.

THE EVIDENCE FOR LITERATE WOMEN IN ANCIENT EGYPT

There is evidence that can be used to show that some women in ancient Egypt were able to read and write, but it is not definitive. The ancient Egyptian word for scribe is *sesh*, and the female equivalent is the word *seshat*. *Seshat* is found as a title in the Middle Kingdom (2055–1650 BCE), but in the context in which the word is found seems to mean a "cosmetician," not a "scribe." The first time the word *seshat* is unquestionably used as a title for a woman who is a scribe is the "Female Scribe of the Divine Adoratrice" Irtyru, of the Twenty-Sixth Dynasty (664–610 BCE), a fact that might have no relevance at all in explaining the use of the title much earlier in ancient Egyptian history. What is interesting is that the ancient Egyptian word *seshat* was also the name of the goddess of writing. If the deity of writing was a female, and was depicted writing in religious scenes, it could hardly have been unusual to have had actual human females writing as well.

Arguments have been made that letters sent by women are evidence of their literacy, but it is really not evidence of anything other than access to someone who could have written the letter. Other evidence that is used to show that women may have been scribes in the New Kingdom (1550–1069 BCE) are Theban tombs that depict a woman sitting with her husband in an offering scene in their tomb. As objects that are placed under chairs are accepted as the property of the person sitting in the chair, the six tombs with scenes of women sitting with scribal equipment under their chairs are interpreted by some scholars as proof that women could be scribes. In one case, which is the most convincing, the wife of the tomb owner is shown four different times in the tomb chapel, and each time she has her scribe's kit with her (Bryan 1985: 23). Unfortunately, the tomb is so damaged that names and titles cannot be seen. In any case, "even if we were to accept all the occurrences of *seshat* as signifying the female equivalent of a male scribe, the number would be pitifully small" (Robins 1993: 113). Women did not have jobs that meant that they had to be scribes, but in certain cases, they could have been taught to read and write at home and be able to make use of this skill without leaving evidence of their literacy behind.

The lady Naunakhte married a "Scribe of the Royal Tomb" named Qenherkhopshef at the village of Deir el-Medineh in the Twentieth Dynasty (1186–1069 BCE). She was apparently young, and her husband was an older man. Qenherkhopsef was the owner of a library of papyrus rolls, and he copied all kinds of documents. One papyrus sheet, for example, known as Papyrus Chester Beatty 3, now in the British Museum (ESA 10685), had a dream book, an interpretation of dreams, on one side, and a poem about Ramses II's Battle of Kadesh, on the other side. These papyri were inherited by Naunakhte and were passed down to her second husband and her children by him, when she died. They were discovered in 1928 in the cemetery at Deir el-Medineh, not in a tomb, but were buried near one of the chapels. It would seem logical in Naunakhte's situation that she might have been taught to read as a child and therefore made a good marital match for an important scribe or that he would have taught her to read once they were married. She clearly valued these papyri after the death of Qenherkhopsef.

Evidence for the education of royal females might be a little stronger. An ivory scribe's palette with the name of the "King's Daughter Meketaten," the second daughter of Akhenaten (1352–1336 BCE), was discovered at the city of Amarna. It had four inkwells, and the colors black, blue, and possibly green or yellow were found in them. The palette itself is only slightly more than five inches long and may have belonged to Meketaten as a young girl. Another ivory palette, belonging to Meritaten, Meketaten's older sister, was found in the tomb of King Tutankhamun (1336–1327 BCE), her brother-in-law. The palette was inscribed with the "King's Daughter Meritaten born of the Great Royal Wife Nefertiti." Meritaten's palette was of normal size and had six inkwells, holding the colors yellow, white, green, black, and red. The argument has been made that because these palettes had colors other than just black and red, they were used for coloring and painting rather than writing. It has been brought up, however, that these two royal princesses may have been schooled in reading and writing but certainly not because they were being trained to be professional scribes. Because their palettes were not standard scribal ones with just black and red ink does not mean that they did not use them to write (Allon and Navratilova 2018: 70–73).

Male tutors, called *mena nesut*, were known for both royal princes and princesses in the Eighteenth Dynasty (1550–1295 BCE). The title for male tutor was the masculine form of the ancient Egyptian word for wet nurse, *menat nesut*. Scholars assume that while the wet nurse literally nursed the royal child, the male nurse functioned as a tutor, teaching reading and writing, among other skills. For example, the royal tutor of Amenhotep II, the son of Thutmose III, is depicted teaching him archery. Undoubtedly, the tutor was also training the child how to behave as royalty. In the beginning, important officials in various positions were given the job of tutor, but later in the Eighteenth Dynasty, tutoring became a career position, and the man holding that job only tutored and worked under an "overseer of tutors."

Probably the best known of these tutors was Senenmut, who was the royal tutor for Neferure, the daughter and only known child of Queen Hatshepsut and her short-lived half-brother and husband, King Thutmose II (1492–1479 BCE). It was probably Thutmose II who appointed Senenmut as the princess's tutor. As well, the king had appointed Senenmut the steward of both the estates of Neferure and that of her mother Queen Hatshepsut. Ten statues have been found that show Senenmut standing and holding a very young Neferure, or sitting with her on his lap. It is extremely unusual in ancient Egyptian art to have a nonroyal and a royal person shown together in statuary. Senenmut seems to have functioned in the capacity of royal tutor until Hatshepsut became king, herself, along with her stepson, Thutmose III (1479–1425 BCE). Then another official, Senimen, became the tutor of Neferure, and Senenmut was in the position of his supervisor (Cline and O'Connor 2006: 98).

HEALTH PROBLEMS IN ANCIENT EGYPT

The environment of the Nile valley created certain health problems for the ancient Egyptians. Everyone lived along a strip of very fertile land on each side of the river, and agriculture was the core of the Egyptian economy. The vast majority of the population were farmers growing emmer wheat and barley. Irrigated land with standing water and wide swaths of grain fields made a perfect environment in which mosquitos could flourish. Nile mud along the edge of the river contained another parasite, schistosomiasis, or bilharzia. Working by or in canals and the banks of the river would have made it impossible to avoid this parasite, especially since most people in ancient Egypt seem to have gone barefoot. In modern Egypt, it is estimated that 20% of the population still suffer from schistosomiasis. Winds would have picked up sand from the deserts on both sides of the river, so the inhalation of sand, which would affect the lungs, was probably impossible to escape.

Understanding the diseases suffered by the ancient Egyptians has constantly changed with advances in modern medical techniques. Two developments, in particular, have been very important for the study of skeletal and mummy remains: the ability to retrieve DNA from ancient viruses and bacteria and the sophistication of tomography or CT scanning. The change in how ancient human remains can be studied, and how our understanding of the health problems of the ancient Egyptians has become so much clearer, can be seen in the various medical studies of the so-called Granville mummy over the past two hundred years.

The Granville mummy is that of an older woman dating to the Late Period (664–332 BCE), named Irtyersenu, that was purchased in Luxor in 1819 and was brought to London. Dr. August Granville unwrapped and autopsied the mummy, publishing a report on it in 1825. A large growth was discovered on one of the ovaries, and Granville pronounced that the woman had suffered from "ovarian dropsy," or cancer, which probably caused her death.

Much later, in 1992, biopsies were done on the mummy, and both carbon and sand particles were found in the lungs. The mummy's muscle tissues showed wasting, so Irtyersenu had probably been ill over a period of time before her death. The ovarian growth found by Granville was determined to have been a benign cyst, so it had nothing to do with her death. The latest study of the Granville mummy in 2009 carried out DNA analysis on tissues from the lung and gallbladder, and lipid biomarker analysis of mycolic acids from the lung and femur was also done. Both these analyses produced evidence of tuberculosis, and it would appear that the cause of Irtyersenu's death was an active tuberculosis infection (Donoghue 2010).

Until recently, paleopathologists had to depend on bone lesions, to identify tuberculosis, although these bone changes could be caused by other conditions as well. In the 1990s, work with ancient DNA began to recover DNA from viruses, bacteria, and parasites, and in 1997, the first *Mycobacterium tuberculosis* DNA sequence was recovered from a New Kingdom mummy from Thebes. This evidence was backed up by a macroscopic examination of the mummy that showed evidence of pulmonary tuberculosis. It has now been shown, through work with ancient DNA recovered from human remains at Abydos and Thebes, that for the period of pharaonic history from the Early Dynastic Period to the Late Period, roughly from 3000 to 664 BCE, the frequency of tuberculosis in Egypt remained at about 25% (Zink et al. 2003: 248). Another result of this DNA work is that different strains of tuberculosis have been distinguished. It has always been assumed that tuberculosis was passed on to the ancient Egyptians from cattle, because cattle were an important part of the ancient Egyptian agricultural economy, and they were slain for temple and funerary food offerings. It is now clear that there was no *Mycobacterium bovis*, the strain of tuberculosis carried by cattle, in ancient Egypt, and so people, not cattle, were the cause of tuberculosis in ancient Egypt.

Evidence for heart disease in ancient Egypt was first recognized in 1852, when artery calcifications were seen in the mummy of an elderly woman. The latest study of heart disease in ancient Egyptian remains, called the Horus Study, started in 2009 and reported on the CT scans of fifty-two mummies, ranging in date from New Kingdom to Roman times (1550 BCE–395 CE). Forty-four of the mummies had "identifiable cardiovascular structures," and twenty of these mummies, or 45%, had "definite or probable atherosclerosis" (Abdelfattah et al. 2013). Calcifications were seen in the arteries of the legs and pelvis and in the aortic and carotid arteries. These twenty mummies had an average age of forty-five years; 55% were male and 45% were female.

One female mummy in the Horus Study supplied evidence that she may have had a prior heart attack. Lady Rai, who died between the ages of forty to fifty, had been a wet nurse in the beginning of the Eighteenth Dynasty and may have taken care of the future King Amenhotep I (1525–1504 BCE). The coronary arteries of Lady Rai could not be seen clearly, but the back wall of her heart had an area of calcification that might have been from a heart attack. Calcifications could also be clearly seen in her thoracic aorta.

The findings of the Horus Study seem to show that in the case of these mummies, atherosclerosis is age related and probably is also related to an upper-class lifestyle, because the people who were mummified were royalty, priests and their families, and high officials. These people most likely did not lead physically active lives, and they would have had regular access to expensive food, such as beef, which is high in saturated fat and raises blood cholesterol. However, further Horus Study's CT scanning of mummies from ancient Peru, the southwest United States, and the late-nineteenth-century CE Aleutian Islands found another answer for heart disease. Atherosclerosis was found in 37% of all these other mummies, and these people were not elite; they were farmers and hunter-gatherers. These people would not have had risk factors leading to atherosclerosis, such as a high-fat meat diet or a sedentary lifestyle, but the risk factors that were part of their daily life were smoke inhalation, chronic infections, and parasites. It has been known for some time that infection and inflammation are risk factors for atherosclerosis, and a recent study also ties air pollution to the risk of developing atherosclerosis.

Ancient Egyptian mummies show extensive evidence of inflammation, infection, and the inhalation of smoke, sand, and rock particles. A CT scan was done of the Late Period mummy of a woman named Asru by the Manchester Museum in 2012. Her only known title was "Lady of the House." Her father was mentioned, and he was called "The Document Scribe of the Southern Region," so her family must have lived a somewhat elite life. It appears that she was probably fifty to sixty years old when she died, and she had osteoarthritis, and in particular, arthritis in her neck. A packet between her legs contained her intestines, which had been removed from her body during mummification. When examined, the intestines produced evidence of parasitic worms known as strongyles. Tissue taken from Asru's lungs showed a cyst, caused by a tapeworm, as well as sand pneumoconiosis, caused by the inhalation of sand particles. Her bladder tissue provided evidence for schistosomiasis, another parasite. Examination of her teeth showed "marked periodontal infection."

So, Asru had ongoing inflammation in her body from three different parasites, gum infections, and sand particles in her lungs. Asru was also found to have calcifications in her aorta and arteries.

If a woman from an upper-class life suffered from these types of medical problems, what did hardworking peasant women suffer from? Unfortunately, only skeletal remains would be found of poorer class people, as they would not have been able to afford to be mummified, and the evidence for medical problems would be limited to what could be found in their bones.

Like heart disease, cancer has always been considered a disease of the modern world, but possible cases of metastatic cancer caused by breast cancer have been reported based on an examination of ancient Egyptian skeletal remains. A skeleton of an older adult female, forty-five years of age, dating to the Third Dynasty (2686–2613 BCE), was found at Deir el-Bersha, with many metastatic lesions throughout her skeleton that indicated breast cancer. Another possible case of metastatic breast cancer was found in the late Old Kingdom cemetery west of the Step Pyramid at Saqqara. An older adult woman, fifty to sixty years old, had an extensive lesion on her right parietal bone and a much smaller cancerous lesion on one of her lumbar vertebrae. In 2015, reports came out describing a late Sixth Dynasty (2345–2181 BCE) female skeleton found at Qubbet el-Hawa in Aswan, displaying skeletal deterioration typical of that caused by the spread of breast cancer. The initial excavation report photos show lesions on a rib, the pelvis, and skull.

There has been extensive recent interest in malaria in ancient Egypt, some of which has come about because of the DNA analysis showing that not only Tutankhamun but also his grandfather, Yuya, and grandmother, Thuya, suffered from *Plasmodium falciparum* infection. Tutankhamun, in fact, had multiple malaria infections. Malaria can also be indicated in skeletons because of the effect of anemia, caused by malaria, on the bones. One scholar has established that 42% incidence of cribra orbitalia, or porous bone tissue in the eye sockets, was found throughout ancient Egypt in all periods, which means that there was always a high prevalence of malaria in the ancient Egyptian population.

Also compelling is the evidence coming out of the cemetery excavations at Tell el-Amarna, where human remains from the North Tombs Cemetery show a malaria rate of slightly more than 70%. The evidence is provided by a new set of criteria for identifying malaria based on skeletal material; five particular skeletal lesions, occurring together, can be indicative of a malaria infection. The skeletal remains in the North Tombs Cemetery are those of laborers and reflect a life of extremely heavy physical work and nutritional deficiency along with suffering from malaria. It is interesting that

75% of the individuals so far found in the North Tombs Cemetery are female, and the highest death rates are at the ages of seven to twenty-four years (Dabbs and Rose 2016: 9). The human remains in these burials seem to suggest that these young people were harshly treated forced laborers.

DOCTORS AND HEALERS

The title "doctor," or *swnw*, in ancient Egypt was known from the beginning of the Old Kingdom around 2686 BCE. In fact, most of the evidence for doctors comes from the Old Kingdom, although there are not that many doctors; only around forty are known. In total, the number of doctors known from all of ancient Egypt were about one hundred. For the most part, these doctors seem to have belonged to the household of a high official or to the royal palace. A number of ranking titles were known for them, such as "Chief Doctor," or "Greatest Doctor of Upper and Lower Egypt." So far, there is no evidence proving that women were ever doctors in ancient Egypt. Clearly, women helped other women in delivering their babies, so the equivalent of midwives existed, but there is no woman that we know of who held the title *swnw*.

There is one woman named Peseshet from the later Old Kingdom (2494–2181 BCE) who holds the title "overseer of the doctors," as well as "overseer of the *ka*-priests of the king's mother." These titles are written on a false door belonging to her and her husband, which was found in part of the mastaba tomb of their son, Akhtihotep, at Giza (Hassan 1932: 83, fig. 143). The son has a number of titles including being a scribe, an overseer of scribes, and an inspector of scribes. He is also an overseer of the *ka*-priests of the king's mother, which is a title held by his mother on her false door as well. Perhaps he inherited it from her. Kanufer, Peseshet's husband, is only given one title on the false door, "royal acquaintance."

Scholars have been disagreeing for years on what this title of Peseshet actually tells us. The word "overseer" is written in masculine form, but the word "doctors" has a "t" that follows it, making it feminine. So, is she an overseer of lady doctors, but overseer was not made feminine?

It is possible, but it is also possible that the "t" was just put in the wrong place. There are a number of feminine overseers, and they all have the correct feminine form of overseer, with a "t" at the end of the word. Furthermore, if Peseshet is an overseer of doctors, does that make her a doctor? That is another question that has to be answered. In any case, if the inscription on her false door is correct in referring to lady doctors, there is no other known evidence for them.

Doctors in ancient Egypt were not known to have the specialties that doctors nowadays have. There were only really two medical specialties: problems having to do with the eyes and intestines. This must indicate that those two parts of the body often had problems. The doctors who specialized in eye problems tended to also be priests of the goddess Sakhmet and were considered to be at a higher rank than a doctor who was a *swnw*. Trachoma, a bacterial infection that can get in the eye from a fly, is a serious problem in modern Egyptian villages and can cause blindness. It must also have been an ancient problem. Ultraviolet light from the sun contributes to cataracts, and that certainly harsh, bright sunlight has always been a problem in Egypt.

Sakhmet was a fierce lion goddess, who was the bringer of plagues and diseases. If Sakhmet could cause these things, she could also keep them from happening, so it was important to worship and appease her. In the Late Period (664–332 BCE), there was a "House of Life" in the temple of Sakhmet at the city of Sais in the delta that seems to have been a center of learning for doctors. A doctor could also carry the title of *sau*, or magician, as when the cause of an illness was not clear, a magical solution was applied. Some doctors also hold the title of dentist along with being a doctor. Another type of healer was the "Controller of Serkhet," a person who treated scorpion and snake bites. Serkhet was the name of the scorpion goddess. Both scorpions and snakes would have been a problem in ancient Egypt and continue to be in Egyptian villages nowadays as they get into houses and sting and bite people.

Doctors, as well as other people in villages who were considered "healers" and called upon to deal with medical problems, were probably fairly competent in dealing with problems that were visible. They knew how to set and put splints on a broken bone, such as an arm. They understood how to stop bleeding, stich cuts, and apply bandages. But, anything internal was not really understood. The ancient Egyptians did understand the beating of the heart and that it could be felt at different places in the body, such as the wrist, because there was a system of channels all through the body, which is explained in the Ebers Medical Papyrus. Other than that, the ancient Egyptians did not seem to have an understanding of the inner workings of the human body, because other substances than blood, such as air, water, feces, and urine, were also believed

A statue of the lion goddess Sakhmet, who was both the bringer of disease and the patroness of healers. She could both destroy and save. (ZzvetDreamstime.com)

to move about in these channels. In fact, lumps and swellings and other similar problems were blamed on unclean material from the intestines traveling in one of these channels to a part of the body it should not be in. As one scholar stated, "This was lowering the blood vessels to the status of sewers" (Majno 1975: 130). The ancient Egyptians did not open up and study the inside of the human body; dissections were not carried out until Greek times in Alexandria about 300 BCE. Although ancient Egyptian doctors are often credited with brain surgery, they did not do any kind of invasive surgery inside the body. There is really no evidence for any kind of surgery other than possibly male circumcision.

THE ANCIENT EGYPTIAN MEDICAL PAPYRI

There are ten medical texts known from ancient Egypt, almost all of which were written during the early New Kingdom. The most famous of these papyri is the so-called Smith Surgical Papyrus, somewhat misnamed as the ancient Egyptians did not carry out surgical procedures, as discussed earlier. The Smith Papyrus was written in the New Kingdom, around 1550 BCE, but because of some of the old words used in the text, the original probably goes back to the early Old Kingdom. It is attributed to an official of King Djoser (2667–2648 BCE) named Imhotep, who was believed to have been the architect of the Step Pyramid Complex. The Smith Surgical Papyrus deals with trauma to the body, and the text begins with wounds to the head and works down, although the text is broken away and stops at wounds and trauma to the chest. Each entry in the text explains the person's wound in detail and then describes how the doctor should treat it, including just making the person as comfortable as possible because death is inevitable. Many of the wounds described are quite serious and seem to be the kinds that would result from an accident at a building site. Moving and setting heavy stones in place at a pyramid must have been quite dangerous. As the architect, Imhotep may well have overseen the treatment of injured workmen at the building site. In much later Ptolemaic and Roman times (332 BCE–395 CE), Imhotep was worshipped as a healer, so there is long tradition that ties him to having been a doctor.

One medical papyrus, the Kahun Papyrus, written in the Middle Kingdom (2055–1650 BCE), is dedicated to female problems. Flinders Petrie found it at the Middle Kingdom town of Lahun in the Fayum in 1889. The text is divided into thirty-four sections, each of which explains a different female physical problem and then states what medical prescription should be used to treat it. The papyrus was broken into pieces, and there are many gaps in the text making it difficult to understand at times. Most of the problems described in the Kahun Papyrus deal with the uterus. Problems and pain in various parts of the body, such as the gums and teeth, as well as legs and buttocks, are blamed on the uterus, which is quite odd, although even in Greek times, female health problems were often blamed on a uterus that had gotten "out of place." Fumigation with incense or smoke, in which a particular substance has been burned, is often what is prescribed for uterine problems. In another medical papyrus known as Ramesseum III, which also has treatments for women, as well as children, incantations are written that must be recited over the prescription or over the patient to whom it is given.

The Kahun Papyrus explains a test that can be done that will show whether or not a woman is able to have a baby. If she puts garlic in her vagina, and she has garlic breath the next morning, then she is fertile. This is based on the idea that an "open" body, one that did not have channels inside that were blocked, would be receptive to sperm, and therefore, the woman could become pregnant. Once again, a test of this type points out the lack of understanding the ancient Egyptians had for the inner workings of the human body.

The Kahun Papyrus gives a "recipe" or a prescription, labeled "Not to become pregnant," and the text that remains says to take crocodile feces and mix it up with fermented dough. The rest of the prescription is broken. Then a second "recipe" mentions putting sodium carbonate or saltpeter in the vagina, and a third "recipe" mentions mixing something with fermented dough and inserting it into the vagina. So, all three of these prescriptions for contraceptives are vaginal suppositories. The same prescription with the crocodile feces and fermented dough is found in Ramesseum Papyrus IV (Riddle 1992: 66–69).

MAGIC AND PRESCRIPTIONS

As the ancient Egyptians had no way to understand and treat a health problem that could not be seen, many health problems had to be treated with magic. For example, in a difficult childbirth, a clay representation of a woman lying in bed with her newborn baby would be put on or near the woman in labor, along with reciting the proper words, to have the actual women become like the representation. If bleeding would not stop, for example, after delivering a baby, an amulet, like the *tyet* of Isis, that looked somewhat like a knot, made of dark red carnelian, could be placed near the bleeding place and a spell would be recited to make the person's blood become hard like the stone of the amulet.

The most commonly worn amulet, for both the living and the dead, was the *wadjet* eye. In the myth of Osiris, when Horus fought his uncle, Seth, to avenge the death of his father Osiris, Horus lost an eye. The *wadjet* eye was the eye Horus needed to become well and whole again, and it was considered to offer protection and health. The *wadjet* eye was added into necklaces and could be worn in the shape of a ring. The *wadjet* eye could be made in a variety of materials, such as faience and gold, as well as in semiprecious stones. Some amulets, such as the *tyet*, needed to be a particular color, but the *wadjet* eye could be any color. Typically, it was out of faience colored blue or green.

A magician was known as a *sau*, and both men and women could be magicians. Priests and doctors could be magicians as well. Magicians made protective amulets for people, spoke or wrote out charms for them, and also mixed prescriptions for health problems.

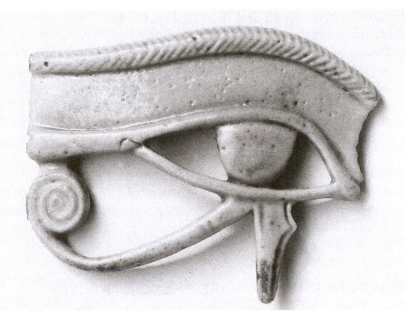

The *wadjet* eye was the most common protective amulet worn in ancient Egypt. It symbolized health and wellness. (The Metropolitan Museum of Art)

The ingredients for a prescription might have to be collected at a certain place at a certain time of the day and have specific spells said, as ingredients were mixed together. The same precautions were taken for the making of an amulet as well. The tying of knots was very important, as knots were considered a barrier that something evil could not pass. Knots could also "catch" something bad, and one treatment for snake bites had to do with tying knots in a particular plant that was then applied to the snake bite to capture the venom. The number of knots was also important, and the number of seven knots appears in many of the magic spells.

Much of the medical care described in the medical papyri was applying the proper prescription to the problem. Prescriptions could have elements of plants, minerals, and animals, cooked, ground, powdered, or soaked. For example, prescriptions for treating blindness tend to contain liver, either to eat or to apply to the eye, or else goose fat, with black-eye paint, or green-eye paint, or red ochre. Headaches often seem to be treated with fish, and in one case a picture of the sun god was to be drawn on linen with the blood of a certain fish and then tied on the head. However, the most common ingredient in ancient Egyptian prescriptions, especially those concerning wounds, was honey. Honey is a mild antibacterial and, if applied to a wound, at least cannot do any harm. Beeswax was also used in some prescriptions. Beer and various herbs and dates were also common. An interesting ingredient for some prescriptions, especially for a cold, and also burns, is milk from a woman who has born a male child, which was considered to be very nutritious and protective. There was even a special pottery vessel made to hold this particular kind of milk. It was made in the shape of a kneeling woman holding a baby, with the spout of the vessel on top of her head. A perfectly preserved New Kingdom example of this vessel is in the Boston Museum of Fine Arts (Accession Number 1985.336).

DENTAL PROBLEMS AND CARE IN ANCIENT EGYPT

Studies of skeletons and mummies show that all ancient Egyptians, from peasant women to queens, suffered from terrible dental problems. It was not cavities that caused the problem, because there were not a lot of sweets in the ancient Egyptian diet, but attrition, or the wearing down of teeth over time. The most important ancient Egyptian food that was eaten on a daily basis was bread. The grain for the bread was ground on a stone with a stone tool, on a floor, which was typically packed dirt. Stone particles and sand during the process of grinding, as well as whatever sand or bits of pottery, got mixed in during the rest of the process of mixing dough and baking it. Wind-blown sand must also have gotten in everything, especially during sandstorms.

The attrition seen on ancient Egyptian teeth is extreme, especially if the person was old. One good example of attrition can be seen in the CT scan of the mummy of a woman named Meresamun, who lived in Thebes around 800 BCE, during the Twenty-Second Dynasty. She was a chantress, or a singer for the god Amun at Karnak Temple, holding the title "Singer in the interior of the Temple of Amun" (Teeter 2009: 21). She must have come from a privileged and important family, as she was buried in a beautifully decorated cartonnage coffin that must have been quite expensive. The CT scan of her mummy showed that all her teeth, all thirty-two of which were present, were "severely worn at the occlusal surfaces (where they meet when biting)" (Vannier 2009: 111, 115, fig. 69). Meresamun is thought to have been around thirty years old when she died. Her teeth were worn down, but not so much that she had begun to suffer from abscesses.

When the cusps of the teeth were worn away, the pulp in the middle of the tooth was exposed. Not only would this have caused terrible pain but it could also bring about infections, and unequal pressure on teeth, that would lead to abscesses. The most serious infections were caused by the root of the tooth becoming infected; this could be fatal if the infection from the root spread. Some mummy CT scans do not find any evidence for a cause of death other than possible dental abscesses. There is a mummy from the Twenty-Second or Twenty-Third Dynasty (945–715 BCE) in the collection of the Walters Art Museum in Baltimore that was discovered in 1930, buried in a ruined part of the funerary temple of Hatshepsut at Deir el-Bahari on the West Bank of Thebes. Information about the mummy is based on CT scans done in 2008, as the mummy is still enclosed in its cartonnage coffin. There is no inscription on the coffin giving a name or title for this individual. She seems to have died between the age of fifty or sixty and had osteoarthritis, which is to be expected at her age. What the CT scans also show is that she had sixteen dental abscesses, and "her death probably resulted from septicemia caused by the abscesses" (Schulz and Seidel 2009: 102). It is interesting that in the place of one missing tooth, a false tooth of resin was put in to fill the gap.

The ancient Egyptian title "dentist" appears for the first time in the Third Dynasty (2686–2613 BCE) tomb of Hesyra at Saqqara. The complete title that he actually has is "Great One of the Dentists and Doctors." There is not a great deal of evidence about what ancient Egyptian dentists could have done for their patients. No particular dental instruments have been found. It appears from prescriptions in medical papyri that treatment was undertaken to keep teeth from being lost, to fill in holes when they were there, and to try and treat the infections and pain. Materials such as flour, honey, and ochre, or else resin would be packed around a tooth to keep it from falling out. Cumin, carob, or willow bark would be applied to heal and control pain. Cinquefoil weed and sweet beer were also prescribed as a mouthwash to lessen pain.

4

PERSONAL PROPERTY

Nefret rolled up the family sleeping mats and piled them against the wall. She took the short reed brush and swept the dirt floor even and smooth again. Going out to the first room of their house, she looked out the small wooden door. Her mother was not yet coming up the street from the pen where they kept their pig. Her father and two older brothers had already left for the South Tombs when the disk of the sun appeared. Her father was a stone cutter, and her brothers hauled away the baskets of chipped stone. Today was the day of the week that Nefret always hated, grinding day—many hours kneeling and grinding enough grain in order to bake bread for the whole week. Her knees and shoulders always hurt, but she didn't want to complain. She wanted to learn to be a weaver, like their neighbor, who made linen cloth and traded it for wheat already ground.

THE ANCIENT EGYPTIAN HOUSE

Archaeologists have excavated ancient Egyptian towns and villages and found remains of fairly well-preserved houses. Although the roofs have collapsed, and the tops of the walls are mostly worn away, the plan of the rooms can be seen, and sometimes objects are still in them. Just like in the modern world, there were large, fancy villas as well as small, cramped houses. The houses themselves, whether large and fancy or government housing, were almost always made out of mudbrick, and the walls were covered with mud plaster. The interior walls could be whitewashed and decorated. The houses were roofed with wood, such as palm or acacia wood, or were covered with other plant materials, such as straw and reeds. Some evidence, such as the remains of a stairway, points to two-story houses, or even three-story, but they may not have been that common. Doors and window frames could be wood as well. Doorsteps, basins, and column bases were stone, but other than that, stone was not used for everyday buildings; stone was used for temples and tombs, as they were to last forever. House floors were generally packed dirt, although in nicer homes, the floor could be done with mudbricks.

A VILLA AT AMARNA

Ancient Egyptian house plans were somewhat standardized, as in all but the smallest houses, there was always a core unit of three rooms arranged in a square that formed the central part of the house. Ancient Egyptian houses were multifunctional, and the largest room of the center part might also have served as the house owner's office. This room was square shaped and the largest room of the house, which is another statement of its importance. Usually, several pillars in the room held up the room's ceiling higher than the ceiling in the rest of the house, so openings or vertical windows let in light and air. Behind the large room was a much smaller room for a bed and another for a bathroom, which is thought to have belonged to the "man of the house." Bedrooms in ancient Egyptian houses can always be recognized by a niche in the room, which marked the space for the bed. Outside of villas at the New Kingdom city of Amarna dating to the reign of King Akhenaten (1352–1336 BCE), and several New Kingdom (1550–1069 BCE) royal palaces, evidence for bathrooms is not preserved. The bathroom was small and lined with plastered walls and with a stone floor. Water had to be brought into the bathroom, and there was a pipe leading from it to the outside of the house where the water could sink into the ground. Wooden toilet seats have been found and may have been placed over pots that were taken out and emptied.

Anyone let into one of these large villas by the front door would have to turn and go through two or three small rooms to reach the large central room, making it a fairly private space. Inside the wall of the house, but outside of the central core of rooms, other rooms were used by the members of the household, as well as the servants and workers who took care of the food and all the other daily chores. Some villas have a second, smaller version of the central core of rooms behind or beside the main one, and this is assumed to have been the wife's bedroom, perhaps for her and the children, although there is no evidence to prove this.

Some studies of the plans of the houses at the city of Amarna have concluded that they "were predominantly two-story buildings" (Spence 2004: 151) and that a second story would have covered approximately 60% of the house. Having a second floor would have moved much of the more private family life upstairs, leaving downstairs for more of the work-based activities. In fact, the study suggests that the upper floor would be planned as an area for women.

VILLAS AT LAHUN AND THEIR DOMESTIC LAYOUTS

Nine very large villas were excavated at the Middle Kingdom (2055–1650 BCE) site of Lahun in the Fayum. They were built on the northeast side of the town, where the land was higher up than the rest of the town, and these elite, and perhaps even royal, villas received the clean and cooling prevailing winds coming from the northeast. Down in the lower part of town were much smaller houses, along with a walled-off portion of the settlement that seems to have been for laborers only. Each of these large villas had a set number of three core rooms. The first in the center part of the house was the reception area/office and private rooms for the man of the house. Alongside that was another similar but smaller unit that could only be entered from the private part of the man's unit. It is thought, therefore, that this unit was for the lady of the house and other family members. On the other side of the man's unit, but with no connecting door from the private part, was a third similar unit. This unit stretched out along the whole side of the house and connected to storage rooms and the granary for the house. This unit also had its own entrance from the outside and was connected only to the outermost of the reception rooms belonging to the man's part of the house. It is thought that the steward of the house and the servants must have lived in this part.

THE TITLE "LADY OF THE HOUSE"

Beginning with the Middle Kingdom and lasting down into Ptolemaic times (332–360 BCE), the most frequently used title for a woman was "Lady of the House"; in ancient Egyptian, *nebet per*. It is assumed that this title was given to the wife of a homeowner, and it implied that she was in charge of the household, whether large or small. However, it is problematic to find archaeological evidence that gives us an idea about the position and status of this woman or what particular rooms or spaces in the house were hers or used by her. Maybe the central core of rooms was just as important to her as to her husband? Maybe she shared this core space with him and it was her sitting place and sleeping place as well? Or, in a very large villa, she may have had a set of core rooms of her own, and her management of the house was carried out from there, just as her husband used his sitting room as an office. Ancient Egyptian villas have been referred to by scholars as "hybrid households" as they were spaces that were both lived in and used for official purposes (Picardo 2015: 244).

Seal impressions of five women with the title *nebet per*, "Lady of the House," were found in association with an area of large villas in the ancient town of Wah-Sut in southern Abydos, dating to the later Middle Kingdom (1870–1650 BCE). A seal impression refers to a piece of mud that has been impressed by a stamp and placed over the opening of a vessel, box, door, linen bag, or a papyrus document. To open the object it is on, it is necessary to break the seal. These seals from Wah-Sut suggest that the women named on them were "in charge of wealth stored in boxes (or behind doors)" (Nelson-Hurst 2017: 136). This wealth could have been jewelry, or possibly expensive commodities like unguents, oils, or other luxury items.

The New Kingdom tomb of Djehuty-nefer at Thebes, Theban Tomb 104, dating to the reign of King Amenhotep II (1427–1400 BCE), is a painting of his multistory townhouse. Djehuty-nefer is depicted seated on a chair in the central large room, while food and drink are being brought to him by a female who is possibly a servant. In another smaller room, he is also shown seated while others are seated on the floor in front of him. The lady of the house does not seem to be depicted, nor are any rooms that may have been hers. The other rooms shown all have servants at work spinning, weaving, grinding, and preparing food. Since the tomb belonged to Djehuty-nefer and the scenes were to present his official life, adding in his wife may have been irrelevant. His wife does appear in religiously related scenes in the tomb, however, such as being seated at an offering table with her husband.

VILLAGE HOUSES AT AMARNA
AND DEIR EL-MEDINEH

Small village houses had three to four rooms. These houses are best preserved at Deir el-Medineh on the West Bank of Thebes and at the workmen's village east of the city of Amarna. This village at Amarna was surrounded by a large square wall, and the houses were arranged in six rows, with five narrow streets in between. The houses all had the same layout of three rooms, the last one of which was divided into two spaces. The first room is thought to be a multiuse family area.

There is evidence in some of these houses that a horizontal loom had been set up in the first room, so the woman of the house must have been involved in weaving, perhaps producing cloth for her own family and trading it with the neighbors as well. Other evidence points to animals kept in the first room and that rather than a roofed room, it was a small unroofed courtyard. In many of the houses, one of the rooms in the back has a blackened wall, so this room must have been the space used for cooking. This would have made the house a very smoke-filled place. Some of the houses, when excavated, seem to have evidence of roof material and oven fragments in the uppermost levels of fill in this back room, suggesting that the material fell down from above. If the woman of the house cooked in an oven on the roof, that would have alleviated the smoke problem. Since the roof and what was on it collapsed down into the room below, evidence for an oven on the roof could be missed, if the excavator was not careful. Early archaeologists tended to clear out rooms, not thinking that the strata inside them were important.

The village of Deir el-Medineh, as it remains now, dates to the Ramesside Period (1295–1069 BCE). It was also a walled village but had a long rectangular shape with one main street down the middle. Approximately seventy houses were built, perpendicular to the street with the house doors all opening onto it. These houses each had four rooms all in a row. First was the outer room with front door to the street. This room often contained a small, rectangular, enclosed platform with several steps leading up to it. It was plastered painted white and commonly decorated with figures of the god Bes, the protector of children and pregnant women. There have been various suggestions put forth for the purpose of this platform; undoubtedly it was associated with the magical protection for newborn babies.

The remains of the New Kingdom workmen's village of Deir el-Medineh on the West Bank of Thebes. (Kar Wai Chan/Dreamstime.com)

The second room always had a dais, probably for sitting on, and a niche for either a stela or an ancestor bust commemorating a deceased ancestor. Because of the sitting area and the special space for ancestor worship and offerings, this room may have been the main family room. This room also had a wooden column in the middle of it that held up a roof higher than that of the other rooms. This allowed vertical window slots to let in air and light. This room also often had a small cellar dug down under it, which was used as a storage space. Beyond the room with the column was another small room that is usually called a bedroom, although that might be a modern interpretation and not correct. At the very back of the house was the kitchen.

THE KITCHEN AND COOKING UTENSILS AND CONTAINERS

A kitchen is usually interpreted as a space for women, and it is assumed that ancient Egyptian women did the daily cooking, just as women do today. When the houses at Deir el-Medineh were excavated, some of the kitchens had a bread oven, a grinding stone, or quern with a handstone. Some of the kitchens even had a small silo, or a large pottery vessel for storing grain or water, still in place.

Cooking pottery was also found in some of the kitchens. Similarly, some houses in the workmen's village at Amarna still had a cylindrical clay oven preserved in the back corner of the house.

It was traditional that women did the grinding of grain for the household. We have written evidence that at the village of Deir el-Medineh, as grinding was considered to be a tiresome chore, servant women were brought in to grind the grain for the households. The two staples of the ancient Egyptian diet were bread and beer. Emmer wheat was ground for making bread, and barley was ground for making both bread and beer. Grinding would have taken a significant number of hours every day. If the grinding was done kneeling down and rolling a handstone on a grinding stone, the work would become very uncomfortable after a time and would have caused skeletal changes in the woman's upper spine, knees, and feet that would have eventually caused pain and discomfort. For that reason, by the time of the New Kingdom, a quern, a sloping stone set up on a platform, was used so that the woman grinding could stand and do the work without the physical discomfort of kneeling. One other problem with grinding grain was that small fragments of stone would get in with the grain, along with sand, which was sometimes added on purpose to break down the grain faster. By eating bread, the ancient Egyptians chewed on sand as well and wore down their teeth terribly. Almost all ancient Egyptians of older adult age suffered from extensive dental problems because of this.

It is usually stated that the kitchen at the back of the house was left unroofed, but it is also possible that early excavators did not recognize that decayed wood or plant material or even bits of clay from plaster could have been from a roof that caved into the room. Some of the kitchens had evidence of stairs that led up either to the roof or possibly to a second-floor room. Clearly, several of the village houses at the workmen's village of Amarna had staircases up to a second floor where the oven was put in order to keep smoke out of the house, but this can't be proven at the village of Deir el-Medineh.

DAILY FOOD AND DRINK

A great deal is known about what food was available to the ancient Egyptians. Food was actually placed in tombs for the deceased to eat in the afterlife, and food was depicted in tomb scenes as well, being prepared and offered to the deceased. The ancient Egyptians believed that the living, the dead, and the divine, all had the same physical needs and needed to eat and drink. The so-called false door of an ancient Egyptian tomb, which was located inside the tomb chapel and "walked" through only by the soul of the deceased in order to receive food in the afterlife, is inscribed with an offering formula that begins: "A thousand of bread, a thousand of beer, a thousand of oxen, and a thousand of geese." Just in case the soul-priestess, or *ka*-priestess, did not come every day with food for the deceased and place it before the false door, the formula itself could magically feed the deceased.

At North Saqqara, archaeologists found a tomb from the time of the Second Dynasty, around 2900 BCE. The burial inside was that of a woman, and they found that an entire set of dishes with food was laid out by her coffin. Based on visual examination, the meal was composed of porridge made from ground barley, a cooked quail, two cooked kidneys, pigeon stew, cooked fish that had been cleaned and the head removed, ribs of beef, small triangle loaves of bread, a small circular cake, stewed figs, and a bowl of berries. As this meal was meant for the afterlife, was this a particularly fancy and extravagant meal, or was it what this woman would have eaten at home?

The main problem about food is that we don't know basic things about how food was prepared, as there are no recipes or cookbooks known from ancient Egypt. It is estimated that only 2% to 5% of the ancient Egyptians were literate, so there was probably no point for written out recipes. People who cooked taught others, just by showing them. Mothers must have had their daughters in the kitchen with them, teaching them how to cook, and so knowledge of meal preparation was passed down through the generations, person to person. We also don't know typical mealtimes in ancient Egypt, or even how many meals a day were eaten. It is logical to think that Egyptians started their day with breakfast. We do know that services in temples, which included feeding the deity, took place three times a day, with the most important service being at dawn, so maybe people ate at dawn as well and then had two more meals later in the day.

The main food and drink that the ancient Egyptian housewife had to prepare and have available every day were bread and beer. The bread could be made of emmer wheat or barley. Wheat made a finer and perhaps more expensive bread, which was round and thin, like modern pita bread. The majority of Egyptians probably ate barley bread more often. This bread was baked in molds and came out cone shaped. Bread was made in various shapes, especially for festivals. It could be sweetened and made into a dessert; honey cake was a special dessert. Honey, figs, and dates were used if anything needed to be sweetened, but probably honey was expensive and not used by most Egyptians.

Beer was made from barley and was very thick, like a soup, and had to be strained before drinking. It was made on a weekly basis, like bread was. It was not as alcoholic as beer is nowadays and was also quite nutritious. Ancient medical texts mention giving this barley beer to women after childbirth in order to build up their strength. Women seemed to have made the beer, perhaps because they also did all the grain grinding, and it was a task that could be done in the house. The production of wine seems to have been a male activity. There is a tomb scene that shows a woman picking grapes along with men, but otherwise scenes of the treading and pressing of the grapes, filling the wine jars, and taking care of the wine cellar all depict men.

It has been said that the typical ancient Egyptian workmen's meal was bread, beer, and onions (Wilson 1988: 21). Was that also what women and children typically ate as a meal? Did families eat together or at specific times? We really don't know. Meals were probably plant based, rather than protein based, because vegetables, lentils, and beans would have been more affordable for most people. Small gardens could have been planted near village houses so that people could grow their own onions, cucumbers, and Romaine lettuce, which were the most common vegetables.

We know ancient Egyptians fished in the Nile, where there were numerous species of fish, mullet, and tilapia being two of the most common fish eaten. Ducks, geese, and pigeon were raised, while wild birds, such as crane and coot, were caught in nets in the swamp. The ancient Egyptians ate the eggs from these wild birds, as the chicken did not appear in Egypt until Ptolemaic times (332–30 BCE). Egyptians also raised pigs, goats, and sheep. Milk from goats and sheep was used to make cheese. Along with fish, pigs were the main source of protein for the majority of the population. Beef was a very expensive, elite protein and also the meat that was offered in temples to the gods and goddesses. Also expensive was wine, which the ancient Egyptians made out of both white grapes and red grapes. In the New Kingdom, there was a second kind of red wine, which until recently had been thought to be made from pomegranates. Tests on the residue in a wine jar from the tomb of Tutankhamun proved that it was made from grapes.

There are some tomb scenes depicting the cooking of meat. It could be grilled on skewers over a fire or else put into a large pot and boiled like stew. We have no idea, however, what was put into the pot with the meat or what types of seasonings, if any, were used. The Egyptians did have onions and garlic, celery, cumin, and fenugreek, as well as herbs and spices, although identifying them by their ancient Egyptian name is often difficult. The only way to keep meat, bird, or fish was to dry it in the sun and pack it with salt.

In the New Kingdom that started around 1550 BCE, Egyptian pharaohs went north into the area of Palestine, Syria, and Lebanon with military expeditions, where they ultimately controlled an empire. The environment of the Northern Empire was very different from that in Egypt, and so the Egyptians of the New Kingdom imported many new foods from the north into Egypt, including apples, dates, pomegranates, almonds, walnuts, sesame seeds, and sesame oil, as well as olives and olive oil. The trees to produce these fruits, nuts, and seeds also became grown in Egypt. The diet of the Egyptians was added to again in Ptolemaic and Roman times when such things as citrus fruits, chickens, and pepper were brought in from India.

FURNITURE

Quite a bit of evidence for furniture has been preserved from ancient Egypt, as furniture was placed in tombs for the deceased to use in the afterlife. Furniture is also shown in many tomb scenes, providing pictorial evidence for furniture use as well. The ancient Egyptians did not have many pieces of furniture in their houses, however. This might have been because Egypt never had the environment in which good wood-bearing trees would grow. The trees used for furniture were mostly acacia and sycamore, which only produce fairly short pieces of timber. Other types of wood, such as cedar, had to be imported from Lebanon and was for the most part used for royal furniture.

There were beds, but they were small and equivalent to the size of what would be a single bed nowadays. The assumption made by modern scholars is that such a bed would have been used only by one person, but that might not have been true. Ancient Egyptian beds had footboards, not headboards. Some beds slanted down so that the foot end was closer to the ground. The "mattress" for the bed was made of fiber, or sometimes leather cords, crossing back and forth from one side of the bed to the other. Two complete and made-up beds with headrests were found in the tomb of Kha and his wife, Merit, at Deir el-Medineh on the West Bank of Luxor. Although this site was a workmen's village, Kha seems to have been a man of some status and wealth. On her bed, Merit had sheets of light linen and a blanket made from heavier linen. Merit would have slept on her side with a U-shaped headrest on a base to hold up her head. The headrest is wrapped with linen to make it more comfortable. Most people probably just slept on a rush or reed mat that was rolled up and put away during the day.

There is usually only one chair found in a tomb, and it seems to have belonged to the man of the house, who was also the tomb owner. One such chair was found in the tomb of Kha and Merit. It was even found with a statuette of Kha standing on the chair, and the chair has two inscriptions giving his name. Also found in the tomb was a small, rectangular, wooden table and four wooden stools, one of which could fold up. A tomb with furniture for the afterlife was probably restricted to fairly well-off officials and their family, and most of the people in ancient Egypt must have sat on mats on the floor, or on a dais, but not on furniture. All these pieces of furniture were built with rather short legs, so that the person sitting on the chair or laying on the bed was much closer to the floor, than in most modern furniture. All furniture was also made out of

A wooden jewelry and cosmetic box from the Eighteenth Dynasty, found in a tomb at Thebes. (The Metropolitan Museum of Art)

wood, although furniture for royalty could also have parts of it in ivory and gold.

People's personal belongings were kept in wooden boxes; there were no drawers, cupboards, or clothes closets in ancient Egyptian houses. Clothing, footwear, jewelry, and toiletry items were all kept in wooden boxes. These boxes could be with or without short legs, and inside these could be divided into compartments designed to hold different objects. These compartments are most commonly found in boxes for jewelry and cosmetics. Jewelry boxes tended to be smaller and much more decorative than the other boxes, and ebony, ivory, and faience were often applied to the wood or used for the handles.

Merit had a rectangular wooden box put in her tomb when she was buried (Vassilika 2010: 51–53). When it was found, the box was still tied closed and sealed with a mud sealing. A short inscription on the side of the box, which must have been added just before her burial, says that it is for Merit's soul. The box was painted with a checkerboard pattern and rows of lotus blossoms and divided into five compartments inside for her cosmetics. She had four alabaster jars, three with covers and one with a little silver handle. She had one unusual jar made out of a horn, with a bronze handle, and one tall-necked faience jar. She also had a dark blue jar with a lid made out of glass, which was rare at that time. Merit also had a blue and yellow kohl tube, also made out of glass with a wooden

A bronze mirror from an early New Kingdom tomb at Thebes. The handle is in the shape of a papyrus plant. (The Metropolitan Museum of Art)

stick to apply the kohl. All these containers were found fitted into the compartments of the box, along with a wooden comb.

Other objects in these types of boxes included mirrors, razors, combs, and tweezers. Metal mirrors are known from the time of the Old Kingdom. A polished copper, or later, bronze, disk was fit onto a wooden, ivory, or metal handle, most commonly made in the shape of a papyrus column but sometimes, especially in the New Kingdom, made in the shape of a standing young woman. The mirror was kept in a slim leather bag to keep it from being scratched. Razors were also made out of bronze, and the thin blade was fit with a wooden or bronze handle. Combs were made in a rectangular shape, with evenly spaced-out teeth. They were most commonly made out of wood, but ivory could also be used.

THE FURNITURE OF QUEEN HETEPHERES

Queen Hetepheres I was the wife of King Sneferu (2613–2589 BCE) and the mother of King Khufu. In 1925, a shaft leading down to a burial chamber (G 7000x) was found on the south side of Khufu's pyramid causeway, just off the northeast corner of one of his queen's pyramids. The objects stacked in the chamber were a canopic chest; two chairs; a bed with headrest; a wooden frame for a canopy over the bed; a wooden carrying chair set on poles; a wooden box for the canopy; vessels of pottery, copper, alabaster, and other stones; bracelets; and cosmetic objects. There was also an empty alabaster coffin with scratch marks on the lid. The wood of the furniture had largely turned to dust, but the gold sheet decoration was preserved and carried the name and titles of Queen Hetepheres on the carrying chair and a jewelry box, and the name and titles of her husband, King Sneferu, were on the poles of the canopy and the box for storing it.

So, what was the queen doing buried in Giza when she should be buried near her husband, King Sneferu, in Dahshur? And where was her body? The excavator George Reisner suggested that the queen had originally been buried at Dahshur, but the burial had been robbed, destroying the queen's mummy. Officials of King Khufu, son of Sneferu, took whatever was left in the tomb and reburied it at Giza, probably not telling the king what had happened to his mother's body. For years, this has been accepted as the explanation, but lately, it has been questioned. It is possible that the queen was originally buried in chamber G 7000x when she died, but then when the small pyramid G1 was completed nearby, her body was moved from the chamber to the pyramid, as the pyramid chamber had been prepared anew with all the funerary goods that she needed.

COSMETICS AND TOILETRIES

Women of all levels of ancient Egyptian society used eyeliner. The black powder known as kohl, which is made from a lead-based ore named galena, helped with the glare of the sun and also was somewhat antibiotic and helped with eye infections. Galena is found in the Eastern Desert, parallel to the area of Upper Egypt. The other color used for eyeliner was green from malachite, which is a copper carbonate and also somewhat antibiotic. Malachite is found in copper ore deposits in both the Eastern Desert and southern Sinai. Green eyeliner was used from earliest times in ancient Egypt, while black eyeliner was more popular beginning in the New Kingdom. Both the kohl and the malachite were ground on a small stone palette, mixed with water or a sticky gum, and were applied to the eyes with a wood or bronze stick, which was rounded at the end. Early containers for eyeliner were little round stone jars, often made out of alabaster. By the time of the New Kingdom, tubes were used instead and were made out of many different materials, including stone, glass, and wood. There could be a single tube with just black eye paint, or two tubes together, one with black and one with green, each with their own stick for applying it. Women also used red ochre mixed with a light grease to rub on their cheeks like rouge, and mixed with oil, red ochre could have been used for lipstick.

Women used both perfumes and oils. Oils, commonly olive oil or almond oil, as well as castor oil and sesame oil, were rubbed on the skin to keep it soft in hot, dry weather. Some of the medical papyri from ancient Egypt include in their prescriptions ways to treat the skin with oils and keep away wrinkles. Perfumes were fat or oil based, impregnated with flowers, leaves, or seeds to give them a pleasant scent. Resins could be used as well. Perfume was rather thick, like an unguent. It was best stored in an alabaster container and was scooped out with large decorative wooden spoons, often with the carved figure of a young woman swimming as the handle.

Perfumes and oils, and the containers and spoons used with them, must have been expensive and must have not been as widely used by women as eyeliner. Moringa oil, for example, was traded into Egypt from northern Syria or Cyprus and apparently was one of the finest and most expensive oils for cosmetics. New Kingdom banquet scenes show elite women with cones of solid perfume on top of their wigs, and as the partying went on, the perfume would melt down into their wigs and clothing.

HAIR AND WIGS

From earliest times, the ancient Egyptians were very concerned about their hair. The excavation of burials in the Predynastic Period cemetery HK43 at Hierakonpolis, dating to around 3500 BCE, discovered many bodies with hair intact. The woman found in burial 16 was about thirty-five years of age, and her shoulder-long hair was not only filled out with false hair extensions but henna had been used as well to dye the hair that had turned gray. A hair problem still found today, lice, was also found in ancient Egyptian hair. Perhaps this is a reason why some ancient Egyptians shaved their head and wore a wig. Women, however, are never shown with a shaved head, like men are. Also, when women wear a wig, their actual hair is often noticeable above their forehead, making it clear that they are wearing a wig. In general, all women in ancient Egypt kept their hair rather long, and elite women had their hair done in elaborate styles that changed through time.

All through pharaonic Egyptian civilization, hairstyles changed continually, as they reflected both social and economic status. Wigs were very common, especially for upper-class women, and were a sign of elite status and worn on special occasions such as banquets celebrating festival days. Wigs were kept in a special tall wooden box that was made just for the wig, in order to keep it clean and undamaged. One such box is known from the tomb of Kha and Merit at the cemetery of the workmen at Deir el-Medineh. Merit's wig was made of human hair and was about twenty inches long. Her wig box opened at the top so that the wig could be lifted out carefully from the wooden bars it hung down from. On the front of the box, just like her cosmetic box, a short inscription had been added that the box with the wig is for Merit's soul.

JEWELRY

Ancient Egyptian women of every class of society wore some kind of jewelry. Jewelry was not only important for adornment but it could also have amuletic power and offer personal protection. Jewelry was worn in life and then placed in burials for the afterlife. The very earliest jewelry known from ancient Egypt are beads of steatite glazed green, which were found in burials of the Predynastic Badarian culture of Egypt, dating to approximately 5500 BCE. Many different stones used in jewelry could be mined in Egypt's Eastern Desert, such as carnelian, feldspar, amethyst, and jasper, and turquoise came from the Sinai Peninsula. Gold was mined in both the Eastern Desert and the Nubian Desert. These materials were expensive and possibly hard for most people to attain, so the ancient Egyptians reproduced the colors of red, blue, green, and yellow in powdered quartz, called faience, which could be heated and molded into any shape and glazed with these same colors.

In the Old Kingdom (2686–2125 BCE), the most common pieces of women's jewelry were bracelets, anklets, and necklaces. The standard colors used followed that of royal court jewelry: gold, blue or green, and red. Gold was the color of the sun, blue was the sky and water, while green was the fertile fields. Red was blood and symbolized life. Although most necklaces worn by women were single strings of beads, the most common necklace in ancient Egypt was the broad collar, composed of multiple rows of beads. The broad collar was worn by both women and men and was also placed on mummies.

In the Middle Kingdom (2055–1650 BCE), scarab rings became very common. Eventually they were made with a bezel so that the scarab could swivel and reveal the person's inscription on the bottom of the scarab, which gave their name and most important title. In this way, a person's scarab ring could be used to stamp and seal various objects. Large numbers of scarab seals and sealings have been found from archaeological sites of the later Middle Kingdom. By the New Kingdom, beginning about 1500 BCE, the scarab ring develops into a solid gold signet ring, which was much more practical for the purpose of sealing. Earrings, studs, and plugs became very popular in the New Kingdom, and these were done in gold, various stones, and also in faience. Simple rings were also done in faience, which was inexpensive and could be used for the equivalent of modern "costume jewelry."

One form of jewelry only worn by elite or royal women was a girdle made out of a string of cowrie shells or gold beads shaped as cowrie shells, which was worn around the hips. Small metal beads would be put inside the shells, and they would make a soft rattling sound as the woman walked. These girdles had religious symbolism and were tied to the goddess Hathor, as the sound made was supposed to be reminiscent of the sound of Hathor, in her form as a cow, coming through papyrus plants in the swamp. Simpler girdles that did not rattle could be worn by dancers or musicians, as is shown in New Kingdom tomb scenes.

CLOTHING AND FOOTWEAR

Ancient Egyptian clothing was made out of linen, which comes from the flax plant. Long fibers are removed from the stems of the flax plant and spun together into a thread that is then woven into a fabric, referred to as linen. Linen could be woven in different weights and could be very soft and thin or else coarse and heavy. Linen was already being produced by the Neolithic Period people living in the Fayum around 5000 BCE. Women in ancient Egypt wore two types of linen clothing, either a dress or a tunic. A dress was composed of a rectangular piece of linen that was wrapped around the body and kept in place by straps, a sash, or a knot. There could be a fringe along the edge of the linen or even colored threads woven into the linen. Tunics were tailored and could have sleeves attached or pleats sewn into the fabric. A woman's tunic "is characterized by its V-neckline" (Vogelsang-Eastwood 1993: 95).

Women also could wear a shawl over a dress or tunic. Some statues, particularly of royal women, depict them completely wrapped in a cloak; this might have been a way to indicate that the woman was old. In art, tunics are shown very slender and tight, so modern scholars often call them "sheath dresses." The depictions are probably idealized, and not realistic, however, because the tunics are shown so tight that it would have been impossible for the woman to walk. Also, many ancient tunics were placed in tombs and so have been preserved, and none of them are very slender. Most ancient Egyptian tunics are "one size fits all," and these are referred to as the bag-tunic, which could be worn by a man, woman, or child of any social status (Vogelsang-Eastwood 1993: 130). The bag-tunic is simply made out of a rectangular piece of cloth folded in half, sewn together on the sides except for holes for the arms, and a hole is cut at the top to put the head through. Many tunics of this style have been found in tombs dating to the New Kingdom.

One last type of dress was not made out of linen but out of beads strung in geometric patterns. The bead dress was known from the period of the Old Kingdom, although there are only a few examples that have been preserved from ancient times. It is not understood if the bead dress was put on so that it was against the woman's skin or was put over a linen garment. It is also not known what the meaning of the dress was or for what particular reason or occasion it might have been worn. The oldest bead dress was discovered in a tomb at Giza in 1927. The tomb dates to the reign of King Khufu (2589–2566 BCE) of the Fourth Dynasty. It is now in the collection of the Museum of Fine Arts in Boston, Massachusetts.

Sandals were the most common type of footwear for everyone in ancient Egypt, although most people probably just went barefoot. Sandals seem to have expressed elite status, in the same way that a wig on a woman expressed elite status. Sandals could be made out of plant fibers, such as palm leaf, reeds, or leather. There does not seem to have been any difference in the sandals for women and those for men; women's sandals just seem to have been smaller. It is clear from tomb and temple scenes, as well as some group statues, that footwear was removed in the presence of someone more important.

DOMESTICATED ANIMALS AND HOUSEHOLD PETS

Village women raised small animals such as sheep, goats, and pigs. At the worker's village at Amarna, there was an area just to the east outside the village wall that clearly had small but walled open spaces and pens for animals. As women were in the village all day, while the men went away to work at various areas of the city of Amarna, the women and children undoubtedly took care of the animals. By the animal pens, archaeologists found remains of limestone, plaster, and pottery water troughs. The bone evidence recovered shows that, in particular, pigs were being raised, fed grain, and also slaughtered, providing meat for the village as well as meat that could be sold.

Written evidence from the village of Deir el-Medineh on the West Bank of Thebes shows that women there took care of cattle or oxen owned by their families, as the workmen would have been away from the village, working at the Valley of the Kings for eight to nine days at a time. The cattle and oxen were not raised for food but to be used for plowing. Some people at Deir el-Medineh did own agricultural land and would have rented a bull, or more probably an ox, to pull the plow, or to thresh the grain. These animals are also shown pulling the sledge with the coffin at funeral processions. Sledges rather than wheeled carts were used because wheels would have been useless in the sand on the West Bank of Thebes.

Actually, wheels were not used by the ancient Egyptians other than on chariots, which had to be driven on fairly hard surfaces. Chariots were specifically for royalty and elite male officials and used in the military beginning in the New Kingdom about 1550 BCE. Women, except for royal women in the Amarna Period (1352–1336 BCE), are never shown in chariots. Donkeys were commonly used to carry heavy loads, and sometimes they are depicted with officials sitting on their back, but women are not shown riding on donkeys or riding on horses. In fact, there is very little evidence from ancient Egypt for horseback riding at all; horses, in teams of two, were instead used to pull chariots.

Royal or elite women could travel in a carrying chair set on poles, which was carried by men, although there is not much evidence for women having a carrying chair. In the Old Kingdom (2686–2160 BCE), for example, only four women appear to have owned carrying chairs, and three of those four women were royalty. Perhaps the most interesting carrying chair scene is in the tomb of the vizier of King Tety of the Sixth Dynasty, Mereruka. He married the oldest daughter of the king, named Waatetkhethor, and she had a section of the rooms in the southwest corner of the superstructure of his mastaba tomb just for herself. In one of her four decorated rooms, a scene of the princess going out in her carrying chair fills the wall. Waatetkhethor sits up in a chair like a throne, with her young son, Mery-Teti, at her feet. The chair is set on long poles being carried not by men but by eight women, four in front and four behind. Her pets, three dogs and a monkey, walk alongside, along with twelve other women, eight of whom are dwarves, carrying boxes and other personal possessions of the princess. The topmost part of the scene is broken, but enough is preserved to show that there was a man walking behind her and holding something to shade Waatetkhethor from the sun.

Travel for any distance was done by boat in ancient Egypt. Canals and the river, not roads, were used. The ancient Egyptians really did not have roads. The idea of travel being tied to water was part of life in ancient Egypt; even the sun god, Ra, was thought to cross the sky every day in a boat. Women are often shown in boats, but they never have a part in sailing or steering the boat; they are always passengers. In fact, there is even a depiction of a royal woman in a carrying chair who has been set down in a boat for a trip on the river.

Dogs and cats must have been present at village communities as either pets or strays looking for food. The evidence for pets comes from tomb scenes and therefore reflects life at an elite level, as most people could not afford a stone-built, decorated tomb. A woman depicted sitting next to her husband in an offering scene in their tomb often has something that belongs to her under her chair. It is frequently a cat, sometimes just sitting, sometimes with a collar and leash tied to the leg of the chair, and sometimes the cat has been given a bone or a fish to chew on. Other times, a vervet or green monkey is shown sitting under or tied to the chair. Both cats and monkeys were accepted, for the most part, as female pets, while dogs, almost always shown with men, were understood as male pets. Dogs are usually depicted in scenes of hunting, a very elite, male sport in which women did not take part. Cats were the sacred animal of Bastet, the cat goddess, who was thought of as nurturing and protective, and were associated with women, children, and the household. Vervet monkeys were also associated with women, and often female cosmetic objects, such as a kohl jar, were made in the shape of monkeys or decorated with the figure of a monkey. There is also a bronze razor with a handle in the shape of a standing monkey (Janssen and Janssen 1989: 51, fig. 13).

5

ENTERTAINMENT

Merit carefully folded her last pleated linen dress and placed it in the box. She would seal the boxes just before her husband's servants came to take them, and take her and her daughter as well, in their carrying chairs. Merit planned to wear one of her best red fringed dresses and of course her longest, curled wig for the short trip through town to Karnak Temple. The wife of Sennefer, Mayor of Thebes could not be seen in just anything! She knew her daughter, Mui-tui, was already packed and set to go. Merit still remembered how excited she had always been as a girl, going off with her mother for their group's month of serving as chantresses in the temple of Amun. How important and grown up she had felt. Merit glanced out of their second-floor window at the wall of Karnak Temple, not far away. Soon she would be in the cool, dark shadows of the inner shrine, and once again she would feel herself gasp as the High Priest opened the naos doors and there he was, King of Gods, Lord of the Thrones of the Two Lands!

MUSICIANS, MUSICAL INSTRUMENTS, AND SINGERS

Music played an important role in ancient Egypt. Music was enjoyed in homes, played for the king and the gods, and played to keep soldiers marching and agricultural workers working. There is a great deal of evidence from ancient Egypt for musicians and their musical instruments, as numerous tomb scenes show both women and men playing musical instruments, and many actual musical instruments have been preserved in the tombs of their owners. Musicians could be professionals, such as the female groups playing the harp, lute, and double oboe at New Kingdom banquets (1550–1069 BCE), or they were people who simply enjoyed playing, such as in the Old Kingdom (2686–2160 BCE) scene in the Saqqara tomb of the Vizier Mereruka, who was shown relaxing on his bed at home while his wife, the princess Waatetkhethor, plays the harp for him.

It must be pointed out, however, that no written musical notation is known from ancient Egypt, so it is difficult to re-create what music from ancient Egypt must have sounded like or what rhythm it had. There is some evidence from the Old Kingdom for "overseers of musicians," who all seem to have been male, although there are females who held titles of "overseer of dancers" and "overseer of singers." The title of "instructor of singers" has been found, which seems to have been only held by men, but there don't seem to be women or men who were instructors of musicians.

The most common of all ancient Egyptian instruments was the harp, which changed its shape and size through time. Women in the later Old Kingdom are shown in tomb scenes playing the harp for members of their family or singing when someone else plays the harp. It has been suggested that at this time, "the performance of music was an integral part of polite society" (Teeter 1993: 87). These types of scenes, particularly the woman playing for her husband, continue into the Middle Kingdom (2055–1650 BCE). By the New Kingdom, beginning in 1550 BCE, there are professional groups of female musicians, either associated with a temple, where higher-status women held the title of "chantress," or in groups, often with dancers, at funerals or memorial banquets held near family tombs.

THE GODDESS HATHOR AND MUSIC

The other musical context women are seen in before the period of the New Kingdom includes religious rituals, particularly for the goddess Hathor, who was associated with music. Hathor's son, Ihy, is referred to as the god of music. He is always shown as a young boy holding a *sistrum*, the shaking instrument that is associated with his mother. In Hathor rituals, shaking and clapping instruments were used; the most important shaking instrument was the *sistrum*, which was basically a large rattle. It had a handle, often decorated with the face of Hathor, surmounted with a rectangular frame, or one curved at the top. In the frame were rows of metal wire strung with metal disks, which would click and clack against each other as the *sistrum* was shaken.

The other shaking instrument, the *menat*, was not really an instrument at all but a necklace of stone or faience beads. It was not worn but rather held in the hand by the metal counterpoise attached to it and shaken so the beads struck each other. The clicking sound of the *menat* and the soft jangling of the *sistrum* were thought to replicate the sound of rustling of papyrus stalks, a sound that pleased and calmed the goddess. From earliest times, Hathor could take the form of a cow and was associated with papyrus swamps. Hathor is often shown as a cow, standing in or emerging from a papyrus thicket.

One of the most famous depictions of Hathor as a cow is a painted limestone statue in the collection of the Cairo Museum (JE 38574–5). The piece was originally set in the chapel of the temple of Thutmose III, set back in the rock of the mountain on the West Bank of Thebes, at Deir el-Bahari. This site had a cult of the goddess Hathor going back to the reign of King Mentuhotep II (2055–2004 BCE) of the later Eleventh Dynasty. The temple was covered by stone debris from an earthquake in early Ramesside times around 1295 BCE, and the complete chapel with the statue in it was discovered in 1906. The cow is shown with papyrus all around her. A statue of the king stands right in front of her, and another depiction of the king is on the cow's side where he kneels and sucks milk from her udder. Hathor was considered the divine mother of the king, and in this statue, her protection and care for her son are emphasized.

Clapping instruments were generally made of hippopotamus ivory and curved following the shape of the tusk. They could also be of wood. The ends, which were clapped together, were decorated with hands and details of the fingers, and bracelets at the wrists were incised into the ivory. Some clappers have a hole at the bottom, and they were tied together so that they could be held in one hand. Quite a number of clappers have been preserved in ancient Egyptian tombs. Clappers were used by magicians to make noise and scare away evil so that they might have been placed in tombs to protect the deceased in the same way.

MUSIC IN THEBAN TOMB SCENES OF THE NEW KINGDOM

There is not very much evidence for women and music in the Middle Kingdom, although scenes in the rock-cut tombs at Beni

Hassan do show women playing the harp with other women singing or sitting down clapping their hands. Much more evidence
exists from the New Kingdom, especially in Theban tombs, where
scenes depict groups of female musicians performing at funerals and religious festivals. The New Kingdom is also a time when
Egypt had expanded its power and created an empire to the north
in the Near East. This contact with different peoples and cultures
brought new plants, animals, and objects of all kinds, including
new and different musical instruments to Egypt.

Theban Tomb 100 belonging to Rekhmire, the vizier of King Thutmose III, has an extensive banquet scene that covers eight registers,
four showing women and four showing men. In the women's part
of the scene, there is a female harpist sitting down playing a ladle-
shaped harp, followed by a woman playing the lute, a woman with
a rectangular tambourine, and then two women who are clapping
and keeping time. In one of the registers above, a woman is tuning
her lute, and in front of her are seated female singers. Below in the
registers of male guests is a male harpist and another man with a
lute. Above them are seated male singers. The difference between
the two musical groups is that the women's musical group has a
tambourine player and female clappers. The festival that is being
celebrated is not clear, but it is not a funeral.

In a slightly later Eighteenth Dynasty tomb, Theban Tomb 52,
belonging to the scribe and priest of Amun, named Nakht, he and
his wife, a chantress of Amun, and guests are shown celebrating
the Beautiful Festival of the Valley. It is a small scene taking up two
registers. One woman stands with a very large boat-shaped harp,
which had come into use by the time of the New Kingdom. Behind
her are two other women, one playing a lute and the other a double
flute. Both the lute and double flute were instruments that came
into Egypt in the beginning of the New Kingdom from Mesopotamia and became very popular.

In the register above the female musicians is a blind man sitting down playing a much smaller ladle-shaped harp and singing.
This specific type of harpist is only shown in some New Kingdom
tombs, and when the decoration of the tomb wall is preserved,
the lyrics written next to the harpist are always the same. Egyptologists have named this the "Harper's Song." Basically, the song
explains that one should enjoy themselves, as everyone will end
up in the cemetery, and no one can get rid of dying. The song also,
however, praises the afterlife and points out that everyone there is
"safe and sound." This song appears to have been one only sung

A facsimile of a banquet scene in the New Kingdom tomb of Nakht, Theban Tomb 52. (The Metropolitan Museum of Art)

by men, and they are almost always depicted as blind. It is possible that being a harpist was one way a blind man could have an occupation. It has also been suggested that the man is shown blind, but perhaps he wasn't. Appearing blind may have been merely symbolic, showing that playing music in a religious setting or ritual did not allow the musician to "see" the god. There are music scenes from the early reign of King Akhenaten at Karnak that show musicians with blindfolds over their eyes when they are playing music. This might be another way of "blinding" a musician so that the god could not be seen. It remains unclear, however, why only a male was ever depicted playing the "Harper's Song" and also why female musicians were never shown blind or blindfolded.

A group of women is seated right behind the blind harpist. They are smelling lotus blossoms and handing mandrake fruits to one another to smell. Mandrake was a hallucinogenic, and both the mandrake and the lotus were sedatives. The smells from these, mixed with drinking wine and beer, would have certainly caused an intoxicated euphoria in which a person could believe that they had communicated with a deity or the dead.

FESTIVALS OF DRUNKENNESS

In the two banquet scenes described previously, there was little or no food in sight. The guests were sitting, holding and smelling blue water lilies, while servants put collars of flowers around their necks and cones of unguents on their heads, as the perfume gave them ritual purity. The servants also brought wine to pour into the drinking bowls of those having wine and vessels of beer for others. Some of the servants held very small jars that apparently contained narcotic substances such as mandrake root, opium, or blue lily. These were added into the wine or beer to increase the effect of the alcohol and also to induce sleep. These festival banquets were not parties to have a few drinks and may be get tipsy. The point of these festivals was to become very inebriated, to the point of gaining an altered state of consciousness, or euphoria. This was a religious or spiritual intoxication that could allow one to have contact with or see a deceased person or a deity. The festival went on all night with guests staying there to sleep and dream of the deceased, or if it was a festival of a goddess, like Hathor, to have an epiphany of the goddess.

The banquet would have taken place in the courtyard right in front of the tomb's entrance to the chapel. The shaft down to the burial chamber would have been out in the courtyard. Early excavators did not pay much attention to the courtyard itself. The pylon-like entrance to the courtyard and the walls must have been in ruins, and the archaeologists just dug away, along with all the other deposits in the courtyard, to reach the shaft opening for the burial and the door for entering the rooms of the painted and decorated chapel. More recent excavations of tombs at Thebes have paid attention to the area outside the tomb door and found blackened areas where offering had been burned, broken pottery from banquet drinking, and plant remains from the flower collars worn by the guests. This is much like what has been found in excavations of the floors of the chapels next to the workmen's village at Amarna.

THE TEMPLE OF MUT AND THE FESTIVAL
OF DRUNKENNESS

The goddess Mut was the wife of the god Amun and the mother of their son, the god Khonsu, the moon god. Both Khonsu and Mut had their own temples, but they were all part of the Karnak Temple complex of the god Amun on the East Bank of the Nile at Thebes. Excavations at the Mut Temple, south of the Amun Temple, in 2004 discovered blocks and columns buried down under the temple floor. The style of the texts on the blocks pointed to the reign of Hatshepsut, and finally five columns were found with the following inscription:

> The King of Upper and Lower Egypt Maatkara. She made (it) as a monument for her mother Mut, the lady of Isheru, making for her a columned hall/porch of drunkenness anew, that she might do "given life like Re forever."(Bryan 2014: 103)

Maatkara is the crown name of Hatshepsut, which translates roughly as "Truth is the soul of Ra." Hatshepsut refers to her mother as Mut, because in the New Kingdom, Amun was accepted as the divine father of the king. Mut first becomes important at Thebes in the earlier part of the Eighteenth Dynasty, during the reign of Hatshepsut. Mut is called "Lady of Isheru" because there is a u-shaped lake that surrounds three sides of her temple, and the lake is referred to as "Ishseru" in ancient Egypt. The meaning of the word is not known, but other temples or chapels for goddesses who could manifest themselves as a feline have this form of lake as well. Mut is most often shown as a woman, but she can also be a woman with a lion's head. Her sacred animal was the cat, which probably explains why Mut is closely associated with two other goddesses: Sakhmet, the lioness, and Bastet, the kitty cat. Hathor can also be a lioness or a cat and associated with Mut.

As Mut became most important during the reign of Hatshepsut, her temple at South Karnak might have first been built in stone at that time. Several statues of high officials who served Hatshepsut were found in Mut's temple, including one of her stewards, Senmut, who was also "Director of the Royal Works at Karnak." It was during Hatshepsut's reign that a processional route was created running south from Amun's Karnak Temple to the Mut Temple. It appears that toward the end of the reign of Hatshepsut's stepson, Thutmose III, the blocks of the porch for the Festival of Drunkenness at the Mut Temple were taken down and used as fill. This fits in with other removal and destruction of Hatshepsut's monuments in order to pave the way for Amenhotep II, son of Thutmose III, to take the throne after his father.

CHANTRESSES OR *SHEMAYIT*

Beginning with the New Kingdom, about 1550 BCE the most common religious title held by a woman was "chantress" or *shemayit*.

It seems that with the disappearance of the title of priestess by the Middle Kingdom, the role of women changed from a priestess who would carry out rituals in a temple to a chantress providing music, singing, and dancing for the temple rituals. Most of the chantresses were attached to the cult of the god Amun, based in Thebes at the temple of Karnak. In the beginning, the title "chantress" was held by elite women married to important officials in the Theban area, but later the title spread and was used by women of lower social class as well. By the time of the Twenty-Second Dynasty, around 945 BCE, the title had mostly disappeared. It is not known what training these women would have had to be a chantress. In some cases, it is clear that the title was handed down from mother to daughter, whereas in others, becoming a chantress seemed to have been a personal decision.

Chantresses were organized into four groups with an overseer for each group. There was a system whereby each group worked in the temple for a month, and then another group rotated in. So, every woman had a month of work and then ninety days when she was back at home again. No matter what god or goddess they served, all chantresses held a *sistrum* and a *menat*, which were the objects used in rituals of Hathor. Their role in the temple was to sing, clap, and sometimes play string instruments to provide music that pleased and satisfied the god or goddess. For example, in Karnak Temple, the chantresses would accompany the High Priest of Amun, or possibly even the king, as he performed the rituals of the care and feeding of the god Amun. This would take place three times a day. As payment, each of the chantresses, like each of the priests, would receive a part of the divine offerings. Since money did not exist in ancient Egypt, salaries were paid in what people need to live on. A chantress would receive grain to make beer and bread, pieces of meat or poultry, as well as fruits and vegetables.

There were women who held the title *hsyt*, or "singer," who were attached to the temple of the goddess Mut in South Karnak. The singers of Mut seem to be much the same as the chantresses of Amun but not with the same status and importance. Other women who held the title of "singer" are shown holding *sistra* (plural of *sistrum*) and *menat* necklaces in processions or celebrations outside of the temple. These women accompanied the god Amun in processions for oracles, in the trip south to Luxor Temple for the Opet Festival, and in crossing the river to the west side of Thebes for the Beautiful Festival of the Valley. The chantresses who had access to the temple had a higher status than the other women who took part in festivities only outside of the temple. Temples were considered to be the house of the god or goddess who lived in it. Therefore, it was private and off-limits for anyone but the highest religious officials and ritualists.

DANCE AND DANCERS

The evidence for dance and female dancers in ancient Egypt comes mostly from tomb scenes that depict a funeral, a funerary ritual associated with the goddess Hathor, or a banquet. There are also relevant titles known at this time held by women who are called "supervisor of the dancers" or "overseer of the dancers." Depictional evidence of dancers in ancient Egypt really begins with the Fourth Dynasty (2613–2494 BCE), particularly in scenes carved in mastaba tombs at Giza and Saqqara. The name *khener* for these dancers starts being used in the Fifth Dynasty (2494–2445 BCE) and signifies that the dancers belong to the cult of the goddess Hathor. The *khener* dancers not only danced but they sang and clapped as well.

Early Egyptological studies interpreted the word *khener* as having to do with women in the royal harem, but this has been shown to be a mistake. In the later part of the Old Kingdom, male dancers joined the *khener*, and men can be found with the title "overseer of the dancers." By the beginning of the Middle Kingdom, around 2055 BCE, only men are "overseers of the dancers" and not women. Societal changes take place between the Old and Middle Kingdoms in which women lose titles giving them control over other people, and instead, women gain a new title "mistress of the house" that proclaims their position as a housewife.

The *khener* dancers can be found in a number of contexts. They can entertain the king, accompany a funeral procession, dance for a god or goddess in their temple, and appear at a childbirth. Some scholars have suggested that dancers in the *khener* also functioned as midwives. In one of the stories of the so-called Westcar Papyrus, which dates from the Hyksos Period around 1650 BCE but is set in the time of King Khufu in the Fourth Dynasty, the wife of a priest of the sun god, Ra, is going to give birth. Ra orders several female goddesses to go and help the birth as the woman is going to have triplets. These babies are actually the sons of Ra, and they will become the next three kings of Egypt. Isis, Nephthys, Meskhenet, and Heket, the female goddesses sent to help, "change their appearance to dancing girls," and when they arrive at the priest's house, they say, "Let us see her. We understand childbirth." Isis says a spell for each baby to slide out easily, and Meskhenet announces for each baby that he is "[a] king who will assume kingship in this whole land" (Lichtheim 1973: 220).

In the Saqqara mastaba belonging to Mereruka, the vizier of King Tety (2345–2323 BCE), there is a section of four rooms just for his wife, the princess Waatetkhethor. She holds titles of "Priestess of Hathor" and "Priestess of Neith" as well as being the "King's eldest daughter." On the north wall of the innermost room, Waa-tetkhethor, whose figure is mostly broken, is seated, watching five registers of female dancers. In the top two registers, pairs of women hold hands and dance together, while two other women standing in each register clap their hands. The bottom three registers all have rows of dancers doing different steps. All the dancers wear a broad collar and a short kilt, and their long hair hangs down behind them, ending in the shape of a ball. There are short phrases in hieroglyphs written between and above the dancers. Not all the words can be understood, but it seems to be a song or chant that has to do with childbirth. Clearly in the next to bottom register, the words above the two dancers leaning far back on one leg are "Behold, it is the secret of birth." In other registers are the words, "come," "hurry," and "pull."

Khener dancers, particularly in the early Middle Kingdom, have tattoos in the form of lines and dashes and dots arranged in the shape of diamonds. The mummies of three women found buried by the funerary temple of Mentuhotep II (2055–2004 BCE) at Deir el-Bahari had tattoos like these. One tomb was undisturbed, and the coffin in the burial chamber held the body of a woman with the titles "Priestess of Hathor" and "Sole ornament of the king." Her tattoos appear to be all dots in lines. Nearby two further burials were found with tattooed women, but they had been badly disturbed, and no textual evidence remained. The woman in Pit 23 had been wearing jewelry around her neck, waist, and wrists, based on impressions left in her skin from beads and residue from silver oxide (Roehrig 2015: 529). She had numerous diamond shapes formed by dots on her chest, the front of her arms, across the front of her abdomen, the front of her thighs, and the top of her feet. The woman from Pit 26 had no evidence of jewelry, same diamond tattoos but fewer of them, and none on her feet. From the broken remains of wooden funerary objects in both pits, as well as a beautiful *sa*, or protection amulet of electrum and silver from Pit 23, along with the location of their burials, clearly these two women held some kind of status in the cult of Hathor or court of King Mentuhotep II. It has been suggested that they are priestesses of Hathor and perhaps were *khener* dancers at the royal court.

There are dolls, called paddle dolls because of their shape, with similar tattoos like those on the women just discussed previously. A large number of these dolls also were discovered in tombs in the same area at Deir el-Bahari as the tombs of the tattooed women. It has been suggested that these dolls represent *khener* dancers, and they have been put in tombs to provide Hathoric dances for the *ka*, or soul, of the deceased (Morris 2011).

OUTDOOR SPORTS

Females in ancient Egypt did seem to take part in activities that would be considered outdoor sports but in a somewhat limited way. There are tomb scenes showing girls and young women throwing and catching a ball, juggling balls, doing somersaults, or practicing acrobatic dance moves. These types of dances would be like those done by the *khener*, just discussed previously. Girls must have learned to swim, as with the nearby Nile River and the numerous canals, the threat of drowning must have been ever present. Swimming, however, must also have been quite dangerous with the presence of hippopotami and crocodiles. There are several references to royal children learning to swim, but it is not clear if that included female royal children.

Females are rarely depicted swimming except on certain cosmetic objects from the New Kingdom (1550–1069 BCE). Cosmetic "spoons," used to scoop up unguents and oils, often have the figure of naked young women, only wearing a bead girdle, stretched out swimming, as the handle, with her arms under the spoon part. The spoon can also take the shape of a bird, with the wings covering the top of the spoon, attached with a peg so that they can be swung open and closed. Beginning in the later Eighteenth Dynasty, love poetry is written, and there is one poem in which a young woman wants to go down to the pond with a young man and wade into the water with him. She says, "Then I'd dive deep down and come up for you dripping" (Foster 1973: 20).

LOVE POETRY OF THE NEW KINGDOM

Three papyri and fragments from a large ostracon, all from Thebes and most probably originally from the village of Deir el-Medineh, have texts that are known as love poems. They date to the Ramesside Period (1295–1069 BCE), are written in the Late Egyptian dialect, and reflect the fact that these texts have been written by well-educated and sophisticated scribes, who were probably men, not women, although who actually composed these poems or songs is not known. The four different sources are Papyrus Chester Beatty 1, Papyrus Harris 500, Papyrus Turin 1966, and Ostracon 25218 in the Cairo Museum. All together they provide more than fifty different "songs" or "recitations." It has been suggested that these poems developed out of songs sung at festival drinking banquets, or they were possibly connected to festivals for the goddess Hathor, where they might have been recited or sung.

At the beginning of each of the poems, the text states, "Beginning of the speech of Entertainment" or "Beginning of the song of Entertainment," so some are clearly to be sung and others to be recited. The evidence seems to show that recited or sung, it was men who were presenting this love poetry. It is also possible that there were musicians who accompanied the song or poem, and they could have been either men or women. It seems clear, however, that the love poetry was meant to be presented publicly at special events and gatherings, not simply read by someone silently.

For the most part, the poems are set outdoors in marshes, gardens, or near bodies of water, and they often make reference to Hathor, or "the Golden One," one of the names given to Hathor, in various ways. Some poems are written from the point of view of the female lover, while others are from the male's point of view. A few examples of beginning lines are as follows: "I love a girl but she lives over there, on the too far side of the river"; "When we kiss, and her warm lips half open, I fly cloud-high without beer!"; and "I just chanced to be happening by in the neighborhood where he lives. His door, as I hoped was open—and I spied on my secret love." (Foster 1974).

CHARIOTS AND WOMEN

Chariots and horses appear in ancient Egypt during the Second Intermediate Period (1650–1550 BCE), when they are brought in by Asiatic invaders known as the Hyksos. The chariot is quickly adopted by the Egyptians. It becomes important for the military and the police, in hunting, and in official transportation in general. The chariot is also something that is basically reserved for royalty and the elite, as to attain and maintain a chariot and horses would have been very expensive. Chariots and horses are only used by men in the New Kingdom, except for the Amarna period, when not only Queen Nefertiti, the wife of King Akhenaten (1352–1336 BCE), and her daughters are seen riding in chariots but the queen herself is shown driving one as well. Blocks from a religious building of Akhenaten at Karnak Temple in Thebes have the remains of a scene of the king riding in a chariot with the queen driving her own chariot behind him. Scenes in elite tombs at Amarna show the king, queen, and their daughters in a chariot together, as well as the king in his own chariot, followed by the queen in hers, and then, behind them, their daughters in chariots along with female attendants and male chariot drivers. It could be that the chariot driver is left out of the scene with the queen to stress her ability and independence, but in any case, at least in the Amarna Period, it was acceptable to have royal females in chariots. There is no evidence for royal or elite females driving or riding in a chariot in any other period of ancient Egyptian history.

These tomb scenes in elite tombs at Amarna also always portray the procession of the royal family down the King's Road from the king's palace residence in the very north of the city to the large temple of the god Aten, the sun disk, in the center of the city. There the entire royal family took part in offering rituals for the god Aten. King Akhenaten made a number of changes to standard ancient Egyptian religion, central to which was his acceptance of the disk of the sun, the Aten, to be his only god. He and his family were the only ones who had access to the Aten, and so they functioned as the intermediaries between Aten and the people. In traditional Egyptian religion, festivals included processions of gods and goddesses out of their temples so that the general population could at least view the closed, small chapel in which a god or goddess's image was kept, as it was being carried by the priests. In this way, people felt that they were part of the festive activities going on. Temples were the private property of deities and closed to everyone other than high priests, so public processions were something very special. King Akhenaten made up for the lack of these processions by allowing the population of his city to view him and his family processing down the royal road on a daily basis.

BOARD GAMES

Board games were as popular in ancient Egypt as they are in modern times. They are found in all types of materials, from beautiful wood for royalty to clay for peasants. The oldest board game known was called *mehen*, the snake game, as Mehen was a snake that guarded the sun god in the underworld. The board game was round and decorated with the coiled body of a snake, with spaces marked off from the tail up to the head, which was in the center. The little square spaces alternated with being a little down or a little up, so there is an interesting pattern to the board. The playing pieces were round, the size of marbles, or else in the shape of small lions. Movement seems to have been decided by throwing sticks. This game was known from the Predynastic Period through to the end of the First Intermediate Period, which is at least two thousand years. Game boards for *mehen* have been found in clay, limestone, wood, and ivory and in different sizes, as well as with differences in the number of spaces a player had to move through to finish.

The most popular game in ancient Egypt was *senet*, or the "passing" game. It was first known in the beginning of the Old Kingdom (about 2686 BCE) and was popular all the way through to the end of the New Kingdom (1069 BCE). In the beginning, *senet* was just a game, but with the New Kingdom, the movement of the pieces on the board became symbolic of the hazardous journey into the afterlife. Playing *senet* against an unknown, invisible opponent, that is, your fate, became the illustration for Spell 17 of the Book of the Dead. The most famous tomb scene that depicts playing *senet* is that of Queen Nefertari in her tomb (no. 66) in the Valley of the Queens.

The *senet* board was rectangular and divided into thirty squares. In the New Kingdom, when *senet* became symbolic of the journey to the afterlife, certain squares were decorated and took on special meaning. The very first square was associated with the god Thoth, because he is the one who leads you to your judgment in front of the god Osiris. The last five squares were all marked with hieroglyphs or depictions. The decoration details on the last five squares can differ somewhat, but usually square 26 says "good," which might mean that the piece can move to the end and finish. Square 27 is marked with water signs, which seems to mean that if a piece lands there, it is removed. The very last square has a depiction of Ra-Horakhty, or the sun god rising on the horizon, reborn, meaning that finishing the game was symbolic of successfully reaching the afterlife.

Senet was played by two people, one with tall pieces that were cone shaped and the other with short pieces that were like spools.

Senet, the most popular board game played in ancient Egypt. (Perseomedusa/ Dreamstime.com)

In early tomb scenes showing this game, each player has seven pieces, but by the New Kingdom, they only use five each. Sticks or bones were thrown to see how far to move, and the players went up and down the board from square one to square thirty. No actual rules have ever been found, but it is possible to figure out most of how the game must have been played.

The *senet* game is made in the shape of a rectangular box, with a drawer that can slide out of one end of the box and that holds the pieces and the throw sticks. The game box can also be turned over, and on the bottom of the other side is the game board for 20-Squares, another very popular game. The same pieces are used as for *senet*, and sticks or knucklebones can be thrown to determine movement. 20-Squares appears to be just a simple and faster version of *senet*, and it became popular beginning in the early New Kingdom, around 1550 BCE.

The last known ancient Egyptian board game is called "dog and jackals," but this is a modern name, as the ancient name is unknown. The most famous example of this game is in the Metropolitan Museum in New York (26.7.1287 a–k). The game board, made out of ivory and ebony, was discovered in a late Twelfth Dynasty (1985–1773 BCE) tomb at Thebes in 1910 and is complete with all its playing pieces. The game board has an odd shape, which has been described as that of an axe-blade or that of a shield. It has a drawer underneath for the playing pieces and is set up on four legs carved in the shape of a bull's legs. The board itself is decorated with a palm tree and has twenty-nine small holes running along each side up to the top of the tree and then back along the trunk of the tree. Two people played the game, one with short pegs that have the heads of dogs and another with tall pegs that have the heads of jackals. Each player had five pegs. The rules are unknown, but sticks much have been thrown and the opponents tried to be the first to get their pegs through all the holes and off the board. This game seems to have only been popular in the Middle Kingdom (2055–1650 BCE) and disappeared after that. Flinders Petrie found a very unsophisticated clay board for "dogs and jackals" at the Middle Kingdom town of Lahun, so it was a game enjoyed by the working class as well as the elite.

TOYS

Identifying a toy in an archaeological context is sometimes problematic. For many years, clay and wood figures of women found in tombs were thought to be toys. Now they are accepted as fertility symbols, and certain ones, which have been called "paddle dolls" because of their shape and decoration, are interpreted as *khener* dancers of the goddess Hathor and are put in the tomb to help with the rebirth of the deceased. Another difficulty is in assigning toys to girls or to boys. Dolls, of course, are always thought to be for girls, while something like a sling shot would be thought of as a boy's toy. These types of interpretations always need to be reconsidered, as modern ideas are much different than ancient ones, and assigning gender roles to ancient people is fraught with modern cultural biases. Objects that are found in settlement contexts that appear to be toys have a better chance of actually being toys than those found in tombs. A number of such objects were found in the Middle Kingdom layer of the town of Lahun by Flinders Petrie in the late 1800s.

There were balls, two made of leather stuffed with grass and two just out of wood. Clay models were found that could have been votives of some kind; one was a boat, although broken, and another a figure of a pig. Small figures, such as crocodiles made out of clay, have been found in settlements, sometimes broken, and often assumed to have been toys. There are magical spells known from ancient Egypt, however, that are to be recited over the figure of a crocodile, which is then to be broken in half. Archaeologists need to be very open-minded, therefore, in certain interpretations of ancient objects.

Some wooden objects with movable parts tied to strings must have been toys. One such toy was found in the Middle Kingdom cemetery at Lisht and is now in the collection of the Cairo Museum. The figures of three dancing dwarves were fit on to a piece of wood. Small holes were cut to insert strings to attach to the bottom of the figures so that they would move when the strings were pulled. Two other movable toys are known from the New Kingdom (1550–1069 BCE) and are in the collection of the British Museum in London. One is a mouse made of clay, with a long thin piece of wood for the lower jaw of the mouse that goes all the way through to the back of the mouse and serves as the tail. The other toy is a walking cat on a base carved in wood. The lower jaw of the cat's mouth is movable, and a string goes from the jaw up through the head so that it can be pulled. It is a carefully done piece with rock crystal set in for the cat's eyes and the teeth are done in bronze. Apparently, this piece was found at Thebes.

The caveat to a discussion of toys in ancient Egypt may be that the idea of special objects made for children to play with might be a rather modern idea. Perhaps play in ancient societies was simply watching what adults did and copying it at a level possible by a child. If children accompanied their parents and joined in, as far as they were able to, what the parent was involved in, not only was the child occupied but was also learning life skills at the same time. Or, perhaps toys were restricted to children from families who could afford toys, as well as afford to let their children spend time playing.

DOCUMENT: QUEEN NEFERTARI, TOMB 66 IN THE VALLEY OF THE QUEENS

On the northwest wall of the first chamber of her tomb, Tomb 66 in the Valley of the Queens, Queen Nefertari, the King's Great Wife of Ramses II, is shown sitting in a pavilion playing senet. The queen holds a sekhem scepter in her right hand, which symbolizes power or control, and with her left hand, she reaches forward to move a piece on the senet board. No opponent sits facing her, because the queen is playing against Fate to be allowed to enter the afterlife and live forever. Just above her the text reads:

The Osiris, the King's Great Wife, Mistress of the Two Lands, Nefertari, Beloved of the Goddess Mut, Justified in the presence of the Great God Osiris.

Spell 17 of the Book of the Dead is written in small vertical columns below the scene. The text in the tomb uses the pronoun "he" rather than "she" in two places. The beginning of the spell with the relevant part about senet *reads:*

Beginning of the praise and recitations of going in and out of the necropolis, of being a blessed one in the beautiful West. Going forth by day, assuming any form he (?) wishes, playing *senet* sitting in a pavilion, coming forth as a living soul, by the Osiris, the King's Great Wife, Mistress of the Two Lands, Nefertari, Beloved of the Goddess Mut, justified after he (?)dies. It is effective for the one who does (this) on earth.

Source: Text translated by Lisa Sabbahy from a photograph of the tomb scene and text.

6

THE LIFE OF
ROYAL WOMEN

In the smaller boat on the canal to the harem in Gurob, she relaxed. Entering into the Fayum, the fields were so green, and palm trees were everywhere. The trip up the Nile from Per-Ramses, the royal residence of her husband, King Ramses II, had been long and tiring. Not that she needed for anything, or had been left alone, as her two favorite court ladies-in-waiting were sent along to take care of her. Everything they needed had been loaded aboard the large riverboat. It was odd to leave the residence, although her husband was very old now, and she hadn't seen him in some time. Such a large family he had, and other queens were so much more important than her. Her son, even almost twenty years later she still thought of him. What would her life have been like had her son lived and grown up to take the throne and rule as the king of Egypt?

THE IMPORTANCE OF THE KING'S MOTHER

Just as royal women in all time periods and civilizations, ancient Egyptian royal women were special and undoubtedly had much more comfortable and secure lives than average ancient Egyptian women. Their importance, of course, was based on the fact that they were related to the king. The king's mother was the most important royal woman of all, because she was the medium who passed on the king's legitimate right to rule. The ancient Egyptian king ruled as a god on the earth, both representing the sun god, Ra, and being his son. The sun god appeared to the king's wife in the guise of her husband and impregnated her. This situation is hinted at in certain titles and symbols, but by the Eighteenth Dynasty (1550–1295 BCE) of the New Kingdom (1550–1069 BCE), there are actually two divine birth scenes known. Perhaps the most famous is that of Queen Hatshepsut in her funerary temple at Deir el-Bahari on the West Bank of ancient Thebes. The other birth scene is that of the slightly later king Amenhotep III and is in the temple of Luxor on the East Bank of Thebes.

Hatshepsut's divine birth scene is done in relief decoration on the south wall at the back of the second terrace of her funerary temple. The scene shows her mother, Queen Ahmose, sitting on a bed with the god Amun-Ra, and two goddesses sit below, holding their feet. Amun-Ra was a composite solar god, who combined a Theban god Amun, with the sun god of Heliopolis, Ra. Amun-Ra was the most important deity of the New Kingdom and was considered the father of the king. In the scene, the god Amun-Ra holds the ankh symbol, the sign of eternal life up to the queen's nose, for her to breathe in, while he also places an ankh symbol in her hand. Then, there is a scene of the god Khnum forming the figure of Hatshepsut on a potter's wheel, along with her *ka*, or soul. In the next scene, the Queen Ahmose, looking pregnant, is led by goddesses into the birthing room, and then at last, Hatshepsut and her *ka* are carried in to be presented to all the assembled gods, as the daughter of Amun-Ra, the future king of Egypt.

THE KING'S WIFE

The king's wife was probably the most important royal woman after the king's mother, because hopefully she would produce his son and heir to the throne. Because of the importance of having a successor, the king of Egypt was polygamous and had many wives. In ancient times, many women died in childbirth, and many more children died before the age of five. The king could marry both within the royal family and women who were not royal. At certain times, such as in the early Old Kingdom (2686–2125 BCE) and the Middle Kingdom (2055–1650 BCE), we know that the king married his sister or half-sister, probably a practical way to keep power and rule within his family line. Marrying a sister also had mythological backing, because the god Osiris, who had been the king of Egypt in the mythical past, had married his sister, Isis, and they produced a son, Horus, who succeeded his father and ruled Egypt.

Every human king of Egypt was considered to be a manifestation of Horus. According to the Heliopolitan myth of creation, Ra created the first brother and sister pair of deities, Shu and Tefnut, and they created the next sibling pair of deities, Geb and Nut, who created Osiris and Isis. So, the son of Osiris and Isis, Horus, was the great-great-grandson of the sun god Ra and son of the king of Egypt, Osiris. The myth, power, and stature of both these great gods back the position and legitimacy of the ancient Egyptian king.

Lana Troy pointed out in her 1986 study of *Patterns of Queenship in Ancient Egyptian Myth and History* that "kingship is a manifestation of the power of the creator, placed in the context of the role of mortal sovereign" (Troy 1986: 2). Since the creator god, Ra, created by himself, he must be androgynous, a mixture of male and female characteristics. As such, kingship, the power of the creator on the earth, must also be both male and female. The king's female relatives, therefore, represent the female half of kingship. In other words, kingship and queenship are the two halves that form divine rule over ancient Egypt.

The role of royal women was based on that of the goddess Hathor, who in mythology could take different forms and be the mother, the wife, or the daughter of the son god, Ra. Hathor was the mother of the young son of the sun, at the same time that she herself was the daughter of the sun god. The generational mother-daughter continuum "functions as the mediator for the transition of the male element from father to son" (Troy 1986: 23). This interpretation explains sibling marriages in the sense that the king would not so much be marrying his sister as he is marrying the female half of his father's renewal and regeneration, and therefore continuing and carrying it on.

TITLES OF ROYAL WOMEN

Royal women had titles that reflected their position and status, and many of these titles have been preserved because they were included in inscriptions carved in stone in their tombs. In the Old Kingdom and Middle Kingdom, royal women could have mastaba tombs, rectangular tombs build of limestone blocks with a chapel in the structure of the tomb, and the burial in a chamber underneath, or they could also have small pyramid complexes. By the New Kingdom, they have rock-cut tombs at Thebes, and beginning with the Nineteenth Dynasty (1295–1186 BCE), the queens are buried in the Valley of the Queens, in the south end of the West Bank at Thebes.

TITLES OF THE KING'S MOTHER

The king's mother had the basic title of "king's mother," often written out in the form "mother of the king of Upper and Lower Egypt." She also held the title "god's daughter," which referred to her father, the deceased king, although this title was only used in the Old Kingdom. Another title only given to the king's mother was "anything she says is done for her," which clearly states the importance and respect she was given. The king's mother wore a vulture headdress, something like a cap, as a symbol of her position. It had the head of a vulture protruding out over her forehead, like the uraeus, the rearing cobra, over the forehead of the king. Vulture feathers spread down the side of her head, along with the legs of the vulture. The talons of the vulture wrapped around the hieroglyphic sign *shen* that has the meaning "to surround" in the sense of protecting. The vulture's tail feathers go down the back of the woman's head in statuary, but when shown in carved relief, they protrude horizontally, like the vulture's head at the front.

Goddesses are often shown with vulture headdresses in the Old Kingdom, so the king's mother might have this symbol because of

A depiction of a king's mother from the early Middle Kingdom, wearing a vulture headdress, a symbol of her position and importance. (The Metropolitan Museum of Art)

its connection with divinity; the title "god's daughter" might have entitled the king's mother to wear a divine headdress. Another reason for the king's mother to take on the vulture headdress is that the ancient Egyptian word for mother was *mwt*, which is written with the hieroglyphic sign of a vulture. The word for vulture is also *mwt*. In the Middle Kingdom and after, all royal women could wear a vulture headdress, so it becomes the symbol of a goddess or royal woman, in general.

Another type of evidence that shows the importance of the mother of the king is that her son could place a statue of his mother in a chapel that he set up for a cult of his statue, to receive offerings, or he could set up a *ka*-chapel, or a "soul"-chapel, just for his mother, where she would receive offerings to sustain her afterlife forever. The king would issue a decree granting that a certain amount of land, an estate or a farm, belonged to the *ka*-chapel, and none of the land, its workers or its animals, could be taxed or taken away or interfered for any reason. See the text of one of these decrees later as Primary Documents.

TITLES OF THE KING'S WIFE

The king's wife, of course, had the basic title "king's wife," or also "king's wife whom he loves," as well as a number of other titles that changed through time. A standard short sequence of Old and Middle Kingdom queen's titles, following "king's wife," were usually "the one who sees Horus and Seth," "great of affection," and "great of praise." The "one who sees Horus and Seth" title is a statement of the fact that the queen is allowed to see the king in divine form, which is what happens when she is impregnated by the god.

In the early New Kingdom, the main and most important queen takes the title "King's Great Wife," which makes her status very clear, and from what we can say she is always the king's first wife. It is also her oldest son, if she has one, who is first in line to take the throne after his father. The queen can also be called "Lady of the Two Lands," which seems to be parallel to the king's title of "Lord of the Two Lands." Undoubtedly, the king's wife had court and religious responsibilities and needed to accompany the king at particular rituals and appearances. It is difficult to say what actual positions or responsibilities a royal wife had other than what would be expected in any family.

By the New Kingdom, the queen has her name in a cartouche, just like the king. A "cartouche" is the word given for the ancient

Egyptian hieroglyphic sign of a cord or rope around something to protect it magically. It is the *shen* sign discussed just earlier, which the talons of the vulture hold in the vulture headdress of the king's mother. The cartouche surrounds and protects the royal name. The New Kingdom queen wears what is standard from now on: the vulture headdress, a modius, or a flat-topped crown, with two long plumes set in it. The queen can also have a uraeus instead of a vulture head over her forehead. By the middle of the Eighteenth Dynasty, the queen could wear a sun disk and two horns on her head, exactly what goddesses wear as well. The queen also holds a fly whisk in her hand, which from this time on can only be held by the queen.

There are a number of titles, perhaps better called epithets, that are given to the queen in the New Kingdom, such as "sweet of love" and "lady of charm." Some of them first appear in the titulary of Queen Neferu, the sister and wife of King Mentuhotep II in the late Eleventh Dynasty. Neferu is called the "lovable possessor of charm" and "pleasing in the columned hall by the smell of her fragrance." Perhaps the most elaborate of these epithets is one given to Queen Nefertiti, the wife of King Akhenaten: "the one who pacifies the Aten with a sweet voice, and in her two hands are the sistra." A *sistrum*, singular, is an instrument that is associated with the goddess Hathor and shaken in religious rituals giving off a rustling, calming sound.

TITLES OF THE KING'S DAUGHTER

The daughters of the king receive the title "king's daughter," which can also be stated as "king's daughter whom he loves" or "king's daughter of his body," which emphasizes that she is really his offspring, as well as "king's eldest daughter," or her title could have all these phrases and be "king's eldest daughter of his body whom he loves." Other than that, a princess in the Old Kingdom could be a priestess of the goddess Hathor or Neith, as could nonroyal women, or even be a priestess of her father, the king. This position would probably entail making offerings to the goddesses and to a statue of the king, perhaps in a daily ritual or on festival days. These priestess titles disappear after the Old Kingdom. In fact, before the beginning of the New Kingdom, priestess titles have disappeared for all women, royal or not.

There is one religious position held by queens, however, that started at the beginning of the New Kingdom. King Ahmose (1550–525 BCE), the first king of the Eighteenth Dynasty, gave his wife,

Ahmose-Nefertari, who was also his sister, a position equal to a high priest at the temple of the god Amun-Ra at Karnak. The title the king gave her was "God's Wife of Amun," meaning that she was the earthly wife of the god. In carrying out the responsibilities of her position, Ahmose-Nefertari first purified herself in the sacred lake that was inside the temple complex of Karnak and then, along with the male high priests, went to the sanctuary to carry out the daily rituals for the god Amun.

The king also endowed her with property, which would have included farmlands with workers and animals, making her a very wealthy woman. Ahmose-Nefertari eventually passed this position on to Queen Hatshepsut when she was married to her half-brother, King Thutmose II. Hatshepsut later gave the position to her own daughter, Neferure, but she died rather young, and the important title seems to have stopped. Much later, in the Twenty-Fifth Dynasty (747–656) of the Late Period, the position of God's Wife of Amun becomes very important again at Thebes, where the God's Wife of Amun, either the king's sister or daughter, was an extremely powerful person.

THE HAREM

Part of the king's palace or royal residence was called the *ipt* or harem, where all the female members of the royal family lived along with all their children. Calling this family residence, a harem, however, should not be understood as a place of seclusion that was guarded and forbidden. It was probably guarded, as the king's palace was, and may have been forbidden except for occupants and their servants but certainly had nothing to do with eunuchs, or veils, or hiding women away. As the king could have different residences, there would have been a number of harems in different locations. There were also, as will be discussed later, harems that were separate institutions of their own.

Harems were for women as well as any of their children. The part of the harem specifically for children was called the *kap*, and non-royal children, particularly sons of important officials, would be raised there along with the royal sons and daughters. The *kap* also seems to have included a school, as it would have been important for royal and elite children to be literate. Growing up in the *kap* is how a young boy from an elite family would start his career in service to the king, as being part of the royal family would make him loyal and devoted to them. There were also young boys from areas outside of Egypt, but controlled by Egypt, who were raised in the *kap* so that they became loyal to Egypt rather than their homeland. This seems to be a practice that began in the reign of Thutmose III (1479–1425 BCE) in the Eighteenth Dynasty. He ordered the rulers of the tribes in Nubia and the cities of Syro-Palestine to send their sons to be raised in Egypt, and when a ruler died, his Egyptianized son was sent to take his place. This guaranteed continued Egyptian political control over these areas.

In the Fourth Dynasty (2613–2494 BCE) of the Old Kingdom, all the most important officials were men who belonged to the royal family, particularly the kings' sons. They were always the viziers and the "overseers of all the works of the king" and filled the other positions that were the most powerful. This situation changes with the following Fifth Dynasty (2494–2345 BCE), when high officials began to be chosen from nonroyal men. It is also the first time that there is evidence that a royal daughter married outside the royal family. The oldest daughter of King Userkaf (2494–2487 BCE) at the beginning of the Fifth Dynasty, Princess Khamaat, was given in marriage to the High Priest of the god Ptah, Ptahshepses. The autobiography that Ptahshepses had inscribed in his tomb describes how he was raised in the *kap* in the royal harem. After this time, it became common for a princess to marry into an elite family, as this practice seems to have become one of the ways that the king was assured loyalty and devotion from his high officials.

Royal females marrying outside the royal family stops with the end of the Old Kingdom, however, and particularly in the following Middle Kingdom, if a princess did not marry her brother, who was the king, she did not marry at all. Why marriage became restricted like this needs much more research about the status of royal women at that time, but it appears that the Middle Kingdom was going back to the practices of the early Old Kingdom, the Fourth Dynasty, when the king emphasized his divinity and power, the royal family was very much on a different level than everyone else, and royal princesses did not marry outside of the royal family.

THE HAREM AT MALQATA: ARCHITECTURE AND DECORATION

There are mentions of the *ipt*, or "harem," of the king in Old and Middle Kingdom texts, but there is no archaeological evidence of a harem, until the New Kingdom reign of Amenhotep III. At this time, the name for harem has changed to *per khenret*, "the house of the harem." There is evidence for a palace of King Amenhotep III (1390–1352 BCE), at Malqata, on the West Bank of Thebes, which includes living quarters for women as well as a separate palace just for his main queen, Great Queen Tiye. In the residential part of the palace, the king has a throne room, with private rooms behind it, including a bedroom and bathroom. On both sides of the columned hallway leading to his throne room are four separate small apartments, which one would assume belonged to female family members. Each of the small apartments has a small entrance hall, off the main columned hallway, a square throne room with four columns, and behind that, two small rooms, a bedroom and a bathroom. There was also a long, narrow room for each apartment, a kind of dressing room, designed to hold boxes with personal possessions and clothing. The ancient Egyptians did not have cupboards and closets, and everything was put into wooden boxes, about the size of a standard modern cardboard box. These boxes, often beautifully inlaid or painted, opened from the top and were used to keep jewelry, toiletries, and clothing.

The palace, as all nonreligious structures, was constructed out of bricks, plaster, and wood, not stone, which was used for temples and tombs, and was meant to last for eternity. Stone was used in the palace for thresholds, column bases, and in bathrooms or slabs on which to set water jars—in other words, places that would have a lot of wear and tear. Enough of the painted plaster from the interior of the palace was found by excavators to be able to reconstruct what the main hallway must have looked like. The columns were wood, cut to look like lotus stalks, and painted blue-green. The plaster on the pavement of the hall was painted much the same color but with ripples like a lake, and fishes were painted on it. There was a black-and-red-patterned dado on the lower part of the wall, and on the upper part, figures of royal women held up offerings in the direction of the king. The wooden ceilings were plastered over and painted with a long line of repeated depictions of the vulture goddess Nekhbet with wings spread out, as if the goddess was flying toward the king on his throne. The main colors throughout the entire hallway were blue, red, and yellow. In the smaller apartments, fragments of plaster were found painted with pictures of calves leaping among plants and birds flying up out of flowers. The decoration was designed to show a world of living creatures and plants flourishing under the rays of the sun and therefore also in the presence of the king, who was the sun god on the earth.

ARCHAEOLOGICAL EVIDENCE
FOR THE HAREM AT GUROB

At the site of Gurob, Mi-Wer in ancient Egypt, in the Fayum, remains were found of a harem that was established in the reign of King Thutmose III in the Eighteenth Dynasty and used till the reign of King Ramses II in the later Nineteenth Dynasty. It is a harem that is completely separate from a royal residence and functioned by itself. Excavations show that there were two rectangular residential structures parallel to each other and surrounded by a wall. Nearby there were workshops, a small settlement, and a cemetery. From the fragments of papyri found at the site, it appears that the women in the harem were weaving very fine "royal linen." There is also archaeological evidence that backs that up. Textile fragments, "spindle-whorls, spinning bowls, and loom equipment," have all been discovered there (Picton 2016: 240). The names and titles of the officials at the harem, the "overseer of the harem," the "deputy of the harem," and the "servant of the harem," all of whom were male, have also been found. The Mi-Wer documents mention a similar harem at Memphis, although it has not yet been discovered, and there is evidence for the titles of an official for a harem at Thebes as well. There were objects found at the Mi-Wer site with the names of Queen Tiye and her husband Amenhotep III, so she may have lived there for some time. Queen Tiye's famous head make from dark wood, now in the Berlin Museum (21.834/17852), came from the site of Mi-Wer.

FOREIGN QUEENS OF THE NEW KINGDOM

In the New Kingdom, beginning with the reign of King Thutmose IV (1400–1390 BCE), it became common for the ancient Egyptian king to request a wife from a Near Eastern ruler. It was a way of bettering foreign relations and keeping the peace, with the caveat that it was a one-way exchange; the king of Egypt never sent one of his female relations to marry a foreign ruler. The first of these marriages seems to have been between Thutmose IV and the daughter of the ruler of Mitanni, in northern Mesopotamia. The marriage is attested in a later letter from the ruler of Mitanni and the Egyptian king. After that, these foreign marriages become more common and are substantiated by much better evidence.

In year ten of his reign, King Amenhotep III married a princess from Mitanni, the area which is now northern Syria. She became his second official wife, after his Egyptian "King's Great Wife," Tiye. The announcement of the marriage was inscribed on a commemorative scarab, of which there are a number of copies. The translated text can be read as a Primary Document below. The most amazing part is that the princess, named Gilukhepa, arrived with an entourage of 317 attendants, servants, and ladies-in-waiting. There must have been an extensive harem building just for this one wife, although no archaeological evidence has been found that would shed any light on this woman's life in Egypt. There is only a letter from her brother, Tushratta, when he was king of Mitanni, late in the reign of Amenhotep III, that he had sent his sister jewelry (Ziegler 2008: 235).

In year thirty-four of his reign, King Ramses II (1279–1213 BCE) married a princess from the land of Hatti in ancient Anatolia, or Turkey, and gave her the title "King's Great Wife." He also gave her an Egyptian name, Maathorneferura, which translates as "she who beholds the falcon king, visible splendor of Ra" (Kitchen 1982: 89). A stela was carved in stone at the temple of Abu Simbel to commemorate the marriage, and there are several small objects that have been found with the name of this queen. It appears that in later years, Maathorneferura lived at the harem in Mi-Wer, because a papyrus found there refers to the fact that the king of Hatti sent linen to her at Mi-Wer (Picton 216: 234).

HAREM CONSPIRACIES

The harem at times must have had numbers of royal wives, all of whom, if they had a son, would have wanted him to be his father's successor. For example, around the pyramid complex of King Pepy I (2321–2287 BCE) of the Sixth Dynasty are seven small pyramid complexes for women who were his wives. There also could have been other wives. That means, at least seven different but related families would have been in the harem, just from those women. King Pepy I complained to his close and loyal official, Weni, that one of his queens had unsuccessfully conspired against him, and he wanted Weni to be very discreet and investigate the matter. Weni explains this in the autobiography in his tomb, but he mentions the queen only with a title and does not give her name. Weni does not give details of what happened, but clearly the problem was taken care of.

Much later, in the reign of Ramses III (1184–1153 BCE) in the Twentieth Dynasty, a rather large conspiracy was put together to assassinate the king, led by a minor wife in the harem, named Tiye.

There is a papyrus in the Turin Museum, known as the Turin Juridical Papyrus, that contains a complete record of the conspirators' trial. Thirty-seven people, along with the minor queen and her son, Pentaweret, were found guilty. Those thirty-seven people got the death penalty, and the son was allowed to "die by his own hand," or commit suicide, but the text does not say what happened to his mother; presumably, as part of the royal family, she received the same punishment. Scholars have always been divided over what may have happened to the king, because the Juridical Papyrus never says what happened to him, although the conspirators mention magic and poison, and one of the guilty men was the king's personal physician. Did Ramses III die in the assassination attempt or sometime later? Finally, in 2012, the mummy of Ramses III had a CT scan done. This showed that under the linen collar that was always wrapped around the king's throat, his throat had been cut completely through back to his cervical vertebrae, killing him instantly.

THE LIFE AND DEATH OF THE KING'S GREAT WIFE, NEFERTARI

Nefertari, the main queen of King Ramses II of the Nineteenth Dynasty, was one of only two queens of ancient Egypt who were deified while they were alive. The other was Queen Tiye, the "King's Great Wife" of King Amenhotep III in the Eighteenth Dynasty. The earliest depiction of Nefertari is of her and her husband in his first year of reign, although there is inscriptional evidence that she was his wife before he was crowned the king. We don't know anything about her origins, although her brother, Amenmose, was the mayor of Thebes, so they must have been from an elite family.

Nefertari held a number of titles that hint at her importance. Her main title was "king's great wife whom he loves," and she was also called "beloved of Mut," who was the divine wife of the god Amun-Ra. She was also called "mistress of the two lands," a title that goes back to the Middle Kingdom, and also "wife of the strong bull," which, of course, reflects her husband's status.

Nefertari gave birth to four sons, the first of whom was the first-born son of Ramses II, Amenherkepeshef. He died as a young boy and was buried in the Valley of the Queens near where his mother's tomb was built. His three brothers also died before being able to take the throne, as their father, Ramses II, lived into his mid-eighties, twice the average life span in ancient Egypt. Ramses II had a second great wife, Iset-Nofret, and it was her son, Merneptah, who finally succeeded his father as king. It is clear that Iset-Nofret was not as important as Nefertari, as she never had a temple built for her, and she was not shown depicted with Ramses II, but Nefertari always was. She was depicted in the Luxor Temple, at Karnak, and also at the Ramesseum, the mortuary temple of Ramses II. Nefertari also had two daughters that we know of, Meryetamun and Nebettawy. Nefertari must have lived in the royal residence at Ramses in the Eastern Delta, but virtually no evidence of her has been discovered there.

Ramses II built two rock-cut temples at Abu Simbel in Lower Nubia, deifying himself as the god Ra in the large, main temple and deifying his wife, Nefertari, as Hathor in the smaller temple. The temple of Ramses II is exactly twice as big as the temple for his wife. On the façade of her temple, however, her standing figures are as big as the ones of her husband standing with her. The temples were built and decorated by the king's regnal year twenty-four, and the royal family traveled from Ramses to Abu Simbel, about a thousand-mile trip, for the ceremonies opening the temples. But Nefertari is not depicted in the reliefs carved at Abu Simbel for this occasion. Ramses II is shown with their daughter, Meryetamun, instead of Nefertari. Perhaps the queen was not well, or perhaps she had already passed away.

Nefertari's tomb in the Valley of the Queens is probably the most beautiful queen's tomb from all of ancient Egypt. It was very badly damaged by rainwater and flooding over the years, as well as being used for numerous burials in later times. The tomb was excavated by Ernesto Schiaparelli of the Turin Museum in 1904, and the wall paintings were restored and repaired by the Getty Museum, from 1986 to 1992. Nefertari was not a king, so she could not have the same religious texts and depictions in her tomb that her husband could have in his tomb. Instead, the painters who did her tomb used inscriptions and pictures from the Book of the Dead that paralleled the inscriptions and scenes that a king would have. The tomb is on two levels; the lower level where her sarcophagus was present was symbolic of the *Duat* or the underworld, the realm of Osiris. The upper level represented the *Achet* or the horizon with the spells that would have the queen transform into a being who could live eternally.

Schiaparelli found Nefertari's damaged granite sarcophagus in the tomb, along with broken pottery jars and wooden furniture. There were thirty-four wooden shabti figures with her name incised on them, a pair of sandals, and two fragments from a mummified leg. In 2016, the leg fragments were scanned and studied. They were judged to belong to an adult female of about forty years of age, which fits about how old Nefertari would have been when she died. In fact, forty was considered old in ancient Egypt. It is assumed from this fact, and the fact that the mummification of the fragments had been very well done, that they probably belong to Neferteri.

ROYAL WOMEN WHO RULED

From earliest times in ancient Egypt, the king's mother was acknowledged as a particularly important person. Some of the kings listed on the Palermo Stone, which is inscribed with annals of the kings of Egypt from the First Dynasty (3000–2890 BCE) through to the middle of the Fifth Dynasty, have their mothers' names written right after theirs, which is a reflection of their status. When Manetho wrote his history of Egypt, *Aegyptiaca*, in the time of Ptolemy II, he added in comments and information along with the king list that he compiled. For the Second Dynasty (2890–2686 BCE), Manetho wrote that women could be king. This much later comment on early Egypt reflects the fact that when the king's son was very young, his mother ruled in his name until he was old enough to rule by himself. Scholars don't know at what age ancient Egyptians considered a child old enough to rule alone but probably around ten to twelve years old. Undoubtedly, there were numerous times when the person functioning as king must have been a woman.

MERETNEITH, FIRST DYNASTY, EARLY DYNASTIC PERIOD

The earliest example known of a mother ruling for her young son was the king's mother, Meretneith, who lived in the First Dynasty (3000–2890 BCE). She was the mother of King Den, who ruled when her husband King Djet died, and her son, Den, was still a young boy. The evidence for this family relationship is based on the fact that Meretneith is named as the mother of Den in the Palermo Stone, and her position as regent for her son seems to be clear by the fact that she was included, with her title "king's mother," in a list of king's names on a clay sealing found at Abydos. Meretneith's tomb was constructed next to that of her husband, Djet, in the royal cemetery at Abydos where only the kings of the first two dynasties were buried. Her tomb was also just northwest of that of her son, Den, and clay sealings with his Horus name were found in her tomb. Like the other royal tombs in the cemetery, Meretneith's tomb had two large stelae with her name on them, set up on the east side of her tomb. There was one difference between her stelae and those of the kings; she did not have her name in a serekh or palace façade design. The serekh façade is a decoration representing the walls of the king's palace and surrounded the Horus name of the king, expressing that "Horus is in the palace." Meretneith did not have a Horus name; her son did, and so her stelae were not decorated with a serekh façade.

Meretneith's burial chamber was cut down into the ground and measures about thirty by twenty-three feet, with eight small, rectangular rooms, probably storage magazines, going all around it. This structure was then surrounded, except on the south corner, by forty-one subsidiary burials. The number of subsidiary tombs is fewer than those around the earlier royal tombs built, but perhaps because Meretneith was technically not a king, she had fewer. These subsidiary burials only appear around the royal tombs of the First Dynasty, and then they stop. They appear to have been human sacrifices, as they are almost all young men in their twenties. They may have been killed to go into the afterlife with the king and continue to serve him. There is no evidence from their skeletal remains as to why they might have been put to death. Like all the other royal tombs at Abydos, Meretneith's tomb also has a separate funerary enclosure, "funerary fort" farther north at Abydos, where rituals and ceremonies of kinship would have been carried out. The enclosure accepted as hers only has slight remains of two of the walls and some of the subsidiary burials. Like the king's tomb, sacrificial burials were also at their "funerary fort."

This evidence for Meretneith's life and her position is not extensive, especially because there is no evidence for her daily life or actions or thoughts. The archaeological and inscriptional evidence is so important, however, because it is the first time there is any kind of glimpse into the members of an early ancient Egyptian royal family, and in particular, evidence of the role of a female member of the royal family.

ANKHENESPEPY II, SIXTH DYNASTY, OLD KINGDOM

Evidence is a little more substantial for Ankhenespepy II, a king's mother of the Sixth Dynasty. She was one of two sisters from

Abydos, in Upper Egypt, whom King Pepy I married. They were the daughters of an elite provincial couple. The marriages have been described as an attempt by King Pepy I to seek out a new base of power with provincial dignitaries who were not from the traditional elite families of the Memphite area, because there had just been an unsuccessful harem conspiracy against the king. It has been suggested, as well, that Pepy I was trying to marry the daughters of trusted and devoted provincial officials, who may also have been related to the king.

Both sisters had the name Ankhenespepy, "May Pepy live for you." Egyptologists refer to the two women as Ankhenespepy I and II. It is often assumed that their names were given to them at the time of their marriage, but there are several examples of nonroyal women with the same name, so it is possible that they were birth names. It is also not clear if the king married them at the same time or separately. Ankhenespepy I apparently married the king first, as she had a son who was older than the son to whom Ankhenespepy II gave birth. Ankhenespepy I's son, Merenra, becomes the king first, and when he dies, Ankhenespepy II's son, Pepy II, becomes the king. This situation is known because it is explained in an inscription found at Abydos, on a stela belonging to the sisters' brother, Djau, who was a vizier in the middle of Pepy II's reign.

After a reign of twenty to twenty-five years, King Pepy I passed away, and his son, Merenra, born to Ankhenespepy I, succeeded him. King Merenra seems to have had a somewhat short rule of perhaps ten years, and then his younger brother, Pepy II, son of Ankhenespepy II, takes the throne. King Pepy II is said to have been six years old when he took the throne, and so his mother, Ankhenespepy II, ruled for him as the regent. A visual statement of her position as regent can be seen in the alabaster statuette in the Brooklyn Museum (39.119), which portrays the queen sitting on a throne with her young son, the king, sitting sideways on her lap with his feet on a second throne, perpendicular to his mother's.

Ankhenespepy II wears a vulture headdress, which in the Old Kingdom signified the queen mother. A small hole above her forehead once held a vulture's head, undoubtedly added in gold, and traces of the vulture's wings can be seen covering her hair. The throne block on which the king puts his feet carries a vertical inscription with his throne name, followed by "beloved of Khnum." This same phrase is written before the name of his mother. The reference to the god Khnum would seem to suggest that the piece came from a temple or chapel at Elephantine, at the border with Nubia, where the cult of Khnum was located, although the provenance of the piece is not known.

There is more evidence for the regency of Pepy II's mother from an inscription at the quarry of Maghara in the Sinai, dating to the fourth year of Pepy II. The complete titulary of the king is given, along with the titles of his mother, who is named both king's mother and king's wife. Her name is followed by a small figure of the queen, who seems to be holding a lotus in one hand and an ankh symbol in the other.

There is no evidence as to how long Ankhenespepy II lived, but when she died, she was buried in a pyramid complex by the pyramid of her husband, Pepy I, in south Saqqara. Her pyramid was much smaller than that of her husband but the largest of the seven queens' pyramids built by Pepy I's pyramid. It was discovered in the year 2000 in the southwest corner of the king's complex. A massive, seventeen-ton, red granite lintel from a doorway into the pillared court of her mortuary temple had been found already. The inscription on the lintel gives her name and title of king's mother on the left side and the name of Pepy II's pyramid on the right. To hold the title "king's mother," her husband, the king, had to die so that the son was king. This means that Ankhenespepy II's pyramid complex was built or at least finished under her son's reign.

Damaged blocks from her mortuary temple have been reassembled into a scene of Ankhenespepy II standing on a skiff and pulling on papyrus stalks in a ritual connected with the goddess Hathor. This type of ritual was restricted to royalty. Ankhenespepy II stands in the boat with her legs apart, not in a way a woman is usually shown in ancient Egyptian art. Legs apart is a male stance, and the king's mother has undoubtedly been given this stance to hint at the fact that she fulfilled a male role in ruling for her son.

Ankhenespepy II's complex has an *antichambre carrée*, normally a space found only in kings' pyramid complexes. It is a square chamber with one central pillar that was always decorated with scenes of gods and goddesses, or divine processions, greeting the king. This is one more hint at the fact that this woman was like a king.

A dark stone sarcophagus was found in the burial chamber with some bones and linen wrapping still in it. The bones, mostly long bones, were those of an older adult female and so very likely belonged to the queen herself. The walls of her burial chamber were covered with Pyramid Texts, with the hieroglyphs retaining traces of green color. Pyramid Texts are spells to aid the king in reaching the afterlife and living forever. They were first put in the pyramid of King Unas at the end of the Fifth Dynasty. Ankhenespepy II's Pyramid Texts are the first ones put into the pyramid of a queen. Once again, this shows the fact that she was like a king and that her son wanted her honored in that way.

HATSHEPSUT, EIGHTEENTH DYNASTY, NEW KINGDOM

Much later in ancient Egyptian history, in the Eighteenth Dynasty of the New Kingdom, a queen named Hatshepsut acted as regent for her husband's son by another wife. Hatshepsut was a royal princess, who had married her brother, Thutmose II. Her husband had another wife, who was not from the royal family, and she bore him a son, also called Thutmose. Thutmose III seems to have been a baby when his father, Thutmose II, died. Hatshepsut served as the regent and, as a contemporary inscription says, "conducted the affairs of the country." For a period of possibly two to seven years, Hatshepsut was content with being regent, and then she took a crown name, in other words, a king's name, and became co-regent with Thutmose III.

Co-regencies were fairly common in ancient Egypt and an accepted way for a king to guarantee that his son and heir would get the throne. The son would be crowned and become king with his father so that two men were actually the king. When the father died, there was no question about the son's position, because he was already king. This is what Hatshepsut did; she became a co-regent. It would seem that this situation, an older female becoming co-regent, must have had the backing of both the royal family and the highest officials in the administration. In fact, most of the officials had served Hatshepsut's father, Thutmose I, and were probably completely loyal to her.

There is some evidence that at the beginning of her kingship, Hatshepsut was depicted with a mixture of clothing and symbols of a queen and a king. Then, probably for state purposes, a change was made, and she was depicted with a male physique and male clothing. It was clear, of course, to everyone that she was actually a woman. Some inscriptions have confusion in the pronouns used, if should it be "he" or "she." One of the officials who went on the military campaign in Nubia with Hatshepsut says in one of his tomb inscriptions, "I followed the good god, King of Upper and Lower Egypt, may she live! I saw when he overthrew the Nubian bowmen" (Redford 1967: 57).

From all the evidence we have, it appears that Hatshepsut was a very effective and able ruler. She carried out an extensive building program at the temple of Amun-Ra at Karnak, including setting up two obelisks. There is evidence that she carried out a military campaign in Nubia. She sent an expedition to the land of Punt to bring back myrrh, incense, and other exotic goods. Her funerary temple at Deir el-Bahari is enormous and beautifully decorated and had been filled with statuary of her as king.

A statue of Hatshepsut as king at her funerary temple at Deir el-Bahari on the West Bank of Thebes. (Ignasi Such/Dreamstime.com)

She and her stepson ruled together for twenty-two years, by which time, by ancient Egyptian standards, Hatshepsut would have been quite old. Based on scans that were done on her mummy, her bones were riddled with cancerous lesions. There is no evidence whatsoever to suggest that Thutmose III might have tried to get rid of his stepmother/ co-regent, and in fact, the lengthy and successful reign that Thutmose III went on to have after she died was probably based on the strong and stable country that she left him to rule.

QUEEN NEFERTITI, WIFE OF THE SO-CALLED HERETIC PHARAOH

Nefertiti, whose name means "the Beautiful One Has Come," married King Amenhotep IV, son of Amenhotep III (1390–1352 BCE), of the Eighteenth Dynasty. Rather than staying and ruling from the capital, Memphis, in the north of Egypt, Amenhotep III lived on the

West Bank of the Nile at ancient Thebes, at a palace complex called Malqata. We don't know if Nefertiti was related to her husband's family, but we do know the name of her wet nurse, which was Tiy, and that the high official Ay, who seems to have been related to the maternal family of Amenhotep IV, was the husband of Tiy.

Amenhotep IV spent five years at Thebes and in that time built eight structures dedicated to the Aten, the physical disk of the sun, who became his new god. During this time, Nefertiti gave birth to two daughters and also was depicted as important in serving the cult of the Aten. Blocks preserved from one of the structures built for the Aten that was called the *Hwt Benben*, or the temple of the sacred benben stone of the sun god, shows Nefertiti, rather than the king, making the offerings to the god, along with her oldest daughter, Meritaten. Other very interesting blocks found at Karnak show Nefertiti alone in a chariot, driving it behind the chariot of her husband. This is the very first time there is evidence for any female to have had anything to do with chariots.

Then, in year five, the king changes his name to Akhenaten, "the one who is useful for the Aten"; closes Karnak Temple; and moves to an empty area in middle Egypt, now referred to as Amarna, or Tell el-Amarna. In a matter of a few years, Akhenaten had built a new city to the god Aten, where he stayed and ruled for about twelve years, until his death, probably in regnal year seventeen. Some scholars think that Nefertiti is the person who ruled after him for a year or two, using the name Neferneferuaten. Then, the boy Tutankhaten becomes king, and Amarna is deserted, as the royal court returns to Memphis, and the new, young king changes his name to Tutankhamun.

In the time at Amarna, Nefertiti gives birth to four more daughters. However, by regnal year fourteen, two of the daughters have died. There are many more scenes in private elite tombs at Amarna of Nefertiti driving her own chariot, and her daughters are also shown in chariots, but they have female attendants with them, and the chariot has a male driver. Nefertiti's famous bust that is in the Berlin Museum was found in the private workshop of the artist Thutmose at his villa in the south of Amarna. The queen is depicted wearing her very unusual high, flat-top blue crown, which might have been her way of having a crown matching her husband's royal blue war crown. It is not known when Nefertiti died. She seems to have had a tomb cut for her in the wadi at Amarna, but there is no evidence of a burial.

DOCUMENT: KING PEPY I, DECREE,
SIXTH DYNASTY

King Pepy I (2321–2287 BCE) of the Sixth Dynasty issued this decree at the time of his heb sed festival, celebrating thirty years of reign. It was found at the temple precinct of the god Min, at Coptos in Upper Egypt, and is now in the collection of the Cairo Museum. It is inscribed on a rectangular stela. In a scene at the top, the god Min faces the king, who extends an offering to him. The king's mother, Iput, stands behind the king, wearing the vulture headdress. The inscription makes clear that no one, even those attached to the royal residence, can take anything from or tax this chapel belonging to her. The text of the decree, slightly damaged in two places, reads as follows:

The Coptite nome, Coptos, the King's Mother Iput's ka-chapel: I have ordered to exempt this *ka*-chapel / / / / / people, large and small cattle, / / / / / any messenger who goes south on any business, My Majesty does not allow any burden to the *ka*-chapel, nor does My Majesty allow the "Following of Horus" to burden it. My Majesty ordered to exempt this *ka*-chapel. My Majesty does not allow to press for any payments for the (royal) residence from this ka-chapel.

Source: Goedicke, H. *Königliche Dokumente aus dem Alten Reich.* Wiesbaden, 1967, p. 43, fig. 4. Translated by Lisa Sabbahy from the hieroglyphic copy.

DOCUMENT: KING AMENHOTEP III,
MARRIAGE PROCLAMATION

This text was inscribed on large, commemorative scarabs issued by King Amenhotep III (1390–1352 BCE), to be sent around the country and proclaim his marriage to the daughter of Shutarna, the ruler of the land of Mitanni, which was called Naharin in ancient Egypt. Six copies of this scarab are known. The top line of the inscription states that it is year ten of Amenhotep III's rule and gives his full titulary as king. Then it continues with the name and parents of his first and "great king's wife" Tiye and then announces the arrival of his foreign wife and her attendants.

Great king's wife, Tiye, may she live! The name of her father is Yuya, the name of her mother is Thuya. The wonders that were brought to His Majesty, may he live, may he prosper, may he be healthy! The daughter of the Great One of Naharin, Shutarna, (named) Gilukhepa. The best of her harem: 317 women.

Source: de Buck, A. *Egyptian Readingbook*. Leiden, 1948, p. 67, 2–5. Translated by Lisa Sabbahy from the hieroglyphic copy.

7

RELIGIOUS LIFE AND THE AFTERLIFE

Ii-Neferti held on to her grandson, Anhotep, and, with her other hand, tapped the ground with a stick to make sure that she wouldn't walk into anything. She couldn't see at all now; she saw darkness by day. Anhotep was leading her to the wise woman to ask what caused her blindness and what she should do. When they arrived, the woman took her by the hand. Ii-Neferti couldn't see the woman, but she smelled the smoke and incense and heard her quiet reciting of spells. Suddenly the wise woman said to her, "[I]t is the Moon, Thoth, the great god who harkens to prayer who makes you see night by day. You must make him a stela and present it with offerings and he will be merciful. But you must stop all this gossiping and quarreling, that is why the god has punished you."

THE MOST IMPORTANT GODDESS IN THE LIFE OF ANCIENT EGYPTIAN WOMEN

Without a doubt, Hathor was the most important goddess for women in ancient Egypt. Hathor was associated with women, love, fertility, childbirth, dancing, joy, playing music, and drinking. Childbirth rituals and symbolism were tied to Hathor. Mirrors and other objects connected with beauty were made with a depiction of Hathor. Love poetry mentions Hathor, mostly referring to her as the "Golden One," perhaps because of her close relationship to the sun god. The Egyptians celebrated a festival of drunkenness, or ecstasy, tied to Hathor every year right before the inundation of the Nile began. But beyond Hathor's importance as a goddess associated with the lives of women, Hathor was of utmost importance in the mythology that backed the Egyptian state and the divinity of the king.

Her name in ancient Egypt was *Hwt-hor*, which literally means the "House of Horus." Horus was the falcon god who ruled Egypt after his father Osiris, the first mythical king of Egypt, was killed by his jealous brother Seth. Isis, of course, was the mother of Horus in the myth of Osiris, but in the mythology of the sun god Ra, Hathor was the wife of Ra, the mother of Horus and therefore the mother of the king. In the modern mind, Horus having different parents might be considered contradictory, but it did not bother the ancient Egyptians. When you died, you went to the afterlife with Osiris, and you rose and were born again every day with Ra; it is just two different ways to explain the same thing. The king was considered to be the falcon god Horus, son of the sun god Ra. Ra and Hathor were thus the parents of the king, and the king and the queen themselves were Ra and Hathor.

Hathor is usually depicted as a woman with a sun disk and horns on her head, but she can also be shown as a cow, which was her animal manifestation. Sometimes just her face is depicted front on, framed by the ears of a cow. Hathor was the wife of the sun god, but she could also be his daughter, and she was a personification of the eye of the sun god. Hathor was close to the goddess Sakhmet, the lion goddess; Bastet, the cat goddess; and Mut, the wife of the god Amun, as well as cobra goddesses such as Meretseger and Renenutet. From the Old Kingdom into the Middle Kingdom, hundreds of women were priestesses of Hathor, and many more were dancers, singers, and musicians in rituals and celebrations for her. Although her main cult temple was at Dendera, north of Thebes, there were many chapels and temples for Hathor throughout Egypt. In fact, the largest of the small temples at Deir el-Medineh was the Hathor temple. King Seti I (1294–1279 BCE), the father of Ramses II, had it built on the north side of the village.

There were also temples of Hathor outside of Egypt proper, as Hathor was thought to be the goddess who protected Egyptians when they went beyond the boundaries of the Nile valley. There is a temple of Hathor at Serabit el-Khadim near the turquoise mines in the southern Sinai, where Hathor was worshipped as the "Mistress of Turquoise." There was also a temple of Hathor as the "Mistress

The temple of the goddess Hathor in the workmen's village of Deir el-Medineh on the West Bank of Thebes. (Bálint Hudecz/Dreamstime.com)

of Byblos" at the Egyptian settlement at Byblos in Lebanon. It could be that Hathor was tied to faraway places because of an important myth concerning her known as the "Myth of the Eye of the Sun" or the "Return of the Wandering Goddess." The story is roughly this: Hathor became angry with Ra and went off to the Eastern Desert, and when Ra wanted his eye back, he sent the other gods after her. Finally, Hathor was persuaded to return and as she traveled back from the farthest reaches of the desert to the Nile valley, all sorts of people and animals joined in and accompanied her. Hathor's return was one of the most important festivals and was celebrated throughout Egypt. Not only on her return did she become pregnant and give birth to the new son of the sun but her return also coincided with the inundation of the Nile and the return of fertility and life to Egypt.

RELIGION IN EVERYDAY LIFE

Archaeological material found in ancient Egyptian houses sheds light on the religious beliefs of the members of the household as well as religious practices that might have been carried out. Most of this domestic religious information comes from two workmen's

villages dating to the New Kingdom (1550–1069 BCE): the workmen's village at the city of Amarna, which was only occupied for
about fifteen years during the reign of King Akhenaten (1352–
1336 BCE), and the village of the workmen who cut and decorated
the royal tombs in the Valley of the Kings, Deir el-Medineh, which
was lived in for the entire period of the New Kingdom. At both
sites, archaeologists discovered small chapels or temples maintained by the villagers, which were seemingly the focus of their
communities. Other evidence of religious beliefs or rituals comes
from objects or decorations found preserved in the village houses.

VILLAGE CULT CHAPELS AT DEIR EL-MEDINEH
AND AMARNA

Both these government villages built for workmen and their
families had temples and chapels built just to the north outside of
their walled village. It is possible that the same people who lived at
Deir el-Medineh were moved to Amarna during the reign of King
Akhenaten, and that is why the chapels at both sites have simi-
larities. It is also possible that these buildings were simply part of
the religious tradition of the ancient Egyptians at that period and
would have existed at many villages; it is only at Amarna and Deir
el-Medineh, however, that they have been preserved.

The chapels all have a similar plan on a straight axis. There is an
outer hall, one or two inner halls, and then at the back the sanctuary, which is usually divided into three parts. Sometimes the
sanctuary is reached by a short flight of stairs. Chapels often have
benches along the walls of the outer hall. Temples, of which there
are two at Deir el-Medineh, never have benches. The chapels were
built from stone, mud brick, mud plaster, and gypsum, and the
halls and sanctuary were roofed with wooden beams, matting, and
plaster.

Kings built two temples and one chapel at Deir el-Medineh, but
there is no evidence of royal construction at the Amarna chapels.
The largest and best-preserved temple at Deir el-Medineh is the
Hathor temple built by Ptolemy IV (221–205 BCE) that replaced and
expanded an earlier Eighteenth Dynasty temple of Hathor. There
is also an Eighteenth Dynasty temple for the god Amun that was
later enlarged by King Ramses II (1279–1213 BCE) and the temple
for Hathor that was built by King Seti I. In total, there were more
than thirty-two temples and chapels built at Deir el-Medineh during the time from the early Eighteenth Dynasty when the village

was founded to the end of the Twentieth Dynasty (1550–1269 BCE), when it was deserted. At Amarna, twenty-three chapels were built during the period of fifteen years when the city of Amarna was inhabited.

At Deir el-Medineh, there is textual evidence that makes it clear that workmen divided into groups, perhaps even family groups, and functioned in the role of priests in these chapels. In some of the chapels, actual limestone seats with names were found. The texts on the seat, along with the person's name, might mention how happy they were to be in the presence of the god, or they use the expression that they are "sitting in the hand of the god" (Sweeney 2014: 226–28). These villagers carried out the cult rituals for the gods or goddesses of the chapels, which in other communities or towns would have used professional priests. Women in the village functioned as singers, as the position of priestess no longer existed in the New Kingdom. Particularly in the temple and the chapel of Hathor, female singers would have had an important role in rituals and at festival times.

The important deities in the chapels at Deir el-Medineh were not only Hathor and Meretseger but also Amun, Taweret, and the deified King Amenhotep I and his mother, Ahmose-Nefertari. Amenhotep I was considered to be the patron saint of the village because it was supposedly during his reign in the early Eighteenth Dynasty that the village was first built. The priests of his chapel carried his statue out in oracular processions where legal problems in the village were decided by the movements of the statue. A full discussion of this oracle can be found in Chapter Two.

Amenhotep I's mother, Ahmose-Nefertari, was one of the most revered queens of the New Kingdom. She was the sister-wife of Ahmose I, holding the title "Great Wife of the King." Ahmose was the founder of the Eighteenth Dynasty, who chased the Hyksos invaders out of the delta and reunited Egypt. Ahmose made his wife part of the cult of the god Amun at Karnak Temple, giving her a new position with the title of "God's Wife of Amun." She was the first person to hold this position, and later, she passed it down to Queen Hatshepsut. Along with this new title, Ahmose-Nefertari was granted estates, with workers and animals, that made her a very wealthy woman. This property was granted forever to the holder of the title "God's Wife of Amun," and the property was passed down from royal woman to royal woman.

Ahmose-Nefertari's second son, Amenhotep I, followed her husband, King Ahmose, on the throne. Amenhotep I was a young boy when he inherited the throne, so his mother served as the regent. This meant that Amenhotep was king, and everything was done in his name, but his mother made all the decisions and was actually ruling for him. She was buried on the West Bank of Thebes, but after the end of the New Kingdom, both her mummy and that of her son were transferred into a cachet for the royal mummies in the cliff above Deir el-Bahari. Her mummy was discovered there in 1818 and is in the Egyptian Museum in Cairo.

Other than for deities, the chapels at Deir el-Medineh were also used for ancestor cults, like those carried on in the village houses with stelae and busts. The chapels had gardens to produce food as well as ovens for cooking. Probably animals for slaughter were kept nearby as well, although archaeological evidence for animals by the chapels has not been found and may have been lost in the first excavations done in the 1920s. In the first hall of the chapels were benches where families could sit and eat as well as set down stelae and ancestor busts.

The twenty-four village chapels found so far at Amarna all seem to have been associated with funerary cults and ancestor worship. Just on the east of the area with the chapels was a small cemetery with a number of burial shafts. The families in the Amarna work-men's village did not have elaborate tombs with courtyards, or large houses, for having banquets, but they had these chapels, probably shared with their neighbors. The chapels had benches on the outer halls for sitting as well as eating, evidenced in some of the halls where seeds and bits of bone were found. There were large jars and T-shaped basins for water, and in annexes to the chapels were pens for animals, such as pigs, based on the bones and coprolites found. There were also areas for slaughtering the animals as well as ovens for cooking. Pottery bowls were discovered with burn marks in them, so incense was being burned. There were also small gardens next to the chapels, or in some cases, the gardens were in an open chapel courtyard. Fragments of leaves and remains of flower heads were also found in some of the chapels, indicating the making of garlands. Scenes in elite tombs of funerary banquets always show the guests wearing floral garlands.

Along with ancestors, there is written evidence from some of the chapels that gods and goddesses were also worshipped. The names of the gods Aten, Amun, Isis, and Shed have been found. Aten was the sun disk, the god whose cult King Akhenaten established, and for whom he built the city of Amarna, or Akhetaten, the ancient

Egyptian name of the city. Shed is a god who appeared during this time. His name means "savior," and people called upon him for help. Shed is a form of the god Horus and is shown as a young man with a bow and arrow and often driving a chariot. These chapels were plastered and painted with religious symbols and designs, although most had been lost except from Chapel 561, the largest chapel, which, for example, has a lotus flower frieze along the top of the walls in the inner hall, vultures with wings spread out in the small hall before the sanctuary, and a panel with winged sun disk in the sanctuary itself. The artistic conventions of the Amarna Period are not apparent in the decoration, however.

THE GODDESS MERETSEGER AT DEIR EL-MEDINEH

Meretseger was a local Theban cobra goddess who was important during the New Kingdom, especially at the workmen's village of Deir el-Medineh. Her name means "She who loves silence," a good name for a snake that is dangerous when bothered. Meretseger was thought to inhabit the mountain on the West Bank of Thebes known as the Peak of the West. At the base of the mountain on the front side facing east was a shrine of Hathor since at least the time of the Sixth Dynasty, so both goddesses were associated with this mountain and with each other.

Certainly, the villagers had to worry about cobras coming into their houses, so worshipping and offering to the snake goddess Meretseger may have been a way to try and pacify her and remove the danger. On the pathway leading from the village of Deir el-Medineh southwest to the Valley of the Queens, there was a rock outcropping that was considered sacred to both the god Ptah and Meretseger. The most important temple for the god Ptah was in Memphis, in Lower Egypt, but since Ptah was the god of craftsmen, it was logical that he was worshipped at Deir el-Medineh, the village of workmen who cut and decorated the royal tombs in both the Valley of the Kings and the Valley of the Queens.

In particular, Meretseger was thought to punish those who had misbehaved in some way, causing them to become ill or blind. To be healed, a villager would set up a stela at the rock sanctuary, where small chambers had been cut into the rock, dedicating the stela to Meretseger and begging for forgiveness. Meretseger was one of the most revered deities in the Theban area, and she was considered to be merciful to those who repented.

THE CONCEPT OF THE AFTERLIFE

The seeming preoccupation that the ancient Egyptians had with death came about from their wish to live forever and to overcome death. They wanted to continue the life that they had on the earth even after they died. This life after death took place in the *Sekhet Iaru*, or the Field of Rushes, which was a copy in heaven of the Nile valley. There, people would spend eternity enjoying abundant fields and with magnificent crops of grain, trees groaning with fruits, and lush and beautiful flowers everywhere. The afterlife reflected their former life on the earth but was perfect, without any toil, trouble, and suffering.

To get into the afterlife, a person would have to be physically and psychologically intact, just like they were in life. This meant that a person had to have their body, their *ka* or soul, and their *ba*, "energy" or "liveliness." A person's *ka* was created at the time the person was, and it was inseparable from them until they died. Your *ka* was like your twin. When you died, your *ka* lived in the "house of eternity," your tomb, and had to be taken care of, just as you had been in life. A contract would be signed with a *ka*-priest or *ka*-priestess who would go to the tomb everyday with food and drink to offer to your *ka*. The priest's or priestess's descendants would inherit the job, theoretically ensuring that someone would bring food offerings to the tomb forever. Although there is evidence of more men serving as *ka*-priests than women as *ka*-priestesses, they were known, and at least two women in the Old Kingdom were overseers of these priests and priestesses.

The offerings for the deceased were placed in the chapel in front of a "false" door—a symbolic door carved in stone and only used by the *ka*, who was able to pass through it. There was also a statue of the deceased in the tomb, referred to as a *ka*-statue that the *ka* could inhabit. The *ka*-statue was placed in a small, enclosed room, called a serdab, often positioned behind the false door. The serdab could also be a separate room with a small vertical opening to let the *ka* look out at the offerings, hear the chants of the priest or priestess, and smell the incense that would be burned.

The *ba* is always shown as a bird. The *ba* left the corpse during the day and flew out of the tomb to soak up sunlight, warmth, and life. It would then return back to the corpse at night and enliven it. Because it was important that the body was preserved and appear lifelike and recognizable to the *ka* and *ba*, the ancient Egyptians experimented with preserving the body, and the practice of mummification developed.

MUMMIFICATION

A body buried in the hot desert sand dries out and becomes naturally mummified. When the ancient Egyptians began to place bodies in tombs, however, they had to counteract decomposition by developing a method of artificial mummification. Mummification was carried out by a special group of priests in a structure that was possibly temporary and set up for the occasion, called the *Per-nefer*, "The Beautiful House." The body was laid on a wooden embalming table, and the brain was removed through a small hole made at the back of the nostrils or else at the base of the skull. Then, certain other internal parts of the body were removed. A cut was made in the lower-left abdomen, and the lungs, stomach, liver, and intestines were taken out. The reason for the immediate removal of these organs was to stop the decomposition of the body. Each one of these organs was embalmed separately and placed in one of the four stone jars, called canopic jars. These jars were, in turn, placed in a canopic box. At the funeral, this box was placed next to the coffin in the burial chamber.

The cavity of the body was then packed with linen and the body heaped with natron, a substance composed mainly of sodium carbonate and bicarbonate. Natron dehydrated the body, removing moisture and fat, so that the body did not decay. After forty days, the natron was removed, and the mummy was washed with palm wine and spices. Then the wrapping ritual began, which took fifteen days if done properly. As the body was wrapped, spells were recited, and various small objects with amuletic powers were placed in the wrappings to protect the body.

Scholars are discovering through CT scans of mummies that not everyone considered elite in ancient Egypt, and discovered buried in well-provisioned tombs, underwent the embalming procedure that was just described. A man named Kha, who seems to have been an architect associated with the tombs at the Valley of the Kings in the period of the reign of kings Amenhotep II to Amenhotep III, was discovered in his undisturbed tomb, Theban Tomb 8, with his wife Merit, in the western cemetery at Deir el-Medineh. In both their mummies, the organs that would normally be removed are present, although, of course, they are desiccated, and no incision to remove their organs can be seen in the lower abdomen of either of them.

Merit's body had been wrapped in many layers of linen that have been tested and show that natron, oils, plant gum, balsam, and beeswax had all been applied to the body or the wrappings. Her mummy was then placed in an anthropoid, or human-shaped, wooden coffin. The top of the coffin was completely covered in gold leaf, and the sides were decorated with gold leaf depictions of deities. This coffin was then placed inside of a larger, rectangular outer coffin, which was completely covered in black bitumen. Merit had a stucco and linen mummy mask over her face and shoulders. It was covered in gold leaf that was then decorated with inlaid glass. On her mummy were gold earrings, a broad collar, a bead necklace, a bracelet, a girdle of gold beads in the shape of cowrie shells, and six gold rings. Merit died when she was about thirty years old, but no evidence for the cause of her death was found.

THE HEART AMULET AND THE BOOK OF THE DEAD

Beginning at the end of the Middle Kingdom, around 1650 BCE, an amulet called a "heart scarab" was first placed on royal mummies, placed over the area of the heart, which was not removed from the body because the heart was thought to be the place of the mind or conscience. The underside of the heart scarab was inscribed with a text from what is known now as the Book of the Dead. The ancient Egyptian name was the Book of Coming Forth by Day, as the spells in it were to make the deceased live again with the rising of the sun each morning. The spells from the Book of the Dead were mostly written on a papyrus roll and placed in the tomb, but the spells could also be painted on tomb walls, or certain spells could be put on particular objects. Book of the Dead papyri appear at the end of the Second Intermediate Period. There were almost two hundred spells that made up the Book of the Dead, many of which had their origin in the Pyramid Texts that appeared in the Old Kingdom reign of King Unas, around 2375 BCE, and the Coffin Texts of the Middle Kingdom (2055–1650 BCE), which developed out of the Pyramid Texts. Not all the spells were always written in copies of the Book of the Dead, although a few spells were essential and appeared in all the copies.

Both men and women could have a copy of the Book of the Dead put in their tomb with them. Someone could buy a prewritten copy with spaces left in certain places for their names to be added in or if one could afford it, request a copy done specifically for them so that their names could be added into the text as it was written and their figures put into some of the vignettes or pictures. Merit, wife of Kha, was not only mentioned in and shown in her husband's Book of the Dead but she had her own copy of the Book of the Dead as well, which is somewhat unusual.

Spell 30B, which ensured that the heart would not testify against the deceased in an important judgment ritual called "The Weighing of the Heart," was put on the underside of the heart scarab. "The Weighing of the Heart" was a ritual that the deceased was believed to go through during the first night after being buried. It took place in front of the god Osiris, the god who ruled the afterlife, and if the deceased passed the "test," they went into the afterlife, joining the god Osiris for eternity. Part of the spell written on the heart scarab reads, "O my heart which I had from my mother . . . Do not stand up as a witness against me, do not be opposed to me in the tribunal, do not be hostile to me in the presence of the Keeper of the Balance!" (Faulkner 1972: 27).

At the Weighing of the Heart ritual, which is depicted in a scene, or a vignette drawn in Spell 125 of the Book of the Dead, the deceased

A "Weighing of the Heart" scene from the Book of the Dead. (The Metropolitan Museum of Art)

had to recite the "Negative Confession" to a group of underworld deities, denying that they had committed any of forty-two different sins in their lifetime. The deceased had to address each god or goddess and then state a particular sin that they did not commit. This confession begins: "O, Far-strider who came forth from Heliopolis, I have done no falsehood. O, Fire-embracer who came forth from Kheraha, I have not robbed. O, Nosey who came forth from Hermopolis, I have not been rapacious" (Faulkner 1972: 31), and so on until the deceased had insisted that they were innocent of all forty-two sins.

After this "Negative Confession," the heart of the deceased was weighed in a scale pan against the feather of Maat, symbolizing "Truth" or "Justice." If the heart of the deceased was heavy with sin, the scale pan with the heart would sink down, and a terrifying creature named Ammit, who had the head of a crocodile, the fore parts of a lion, and the hind parts of a hippopotamus, would gobble up the heart, thus destroying the physical completeness of the deceased and ending their chance to live again in the afterlife. If the deceased was not physically and psychologically complete in the way they were on the earth, they could not enter the afterlife and live again; the ancient Egyptians referred to this as the "Second Death."

THE FUNERAL

When the wrapping of the body was completed, the deceased was handed back to their family for the funeral. A procession, the size and extravagance of which would have depended on the wealth of the deceased, would take the mummy to the tomb. Depictions of New Kingdom (1550–1069 BCE) funeral processions at Thebes always show the crossing of the Nile, going from the east to the west side, as the town of Thebes was on the east side and the necropolis with the tombs on the west. The crossing of the Nile was done by boat, and then the deceased would be dragged to the tomb on a sled pulled by oxen or cattle, accompanied by men carrying the possessions of the deceased that would be placed in the tomb.

Mourners would also accompany the procession, along with two women who played the roles of the goddesses Isis and Nephthys, the two sisters of Osiris, who, in ancient Egyptian mythology, were responsible for protecting the body of Osiris and burying him. These two goddesses were referred to as the *djerty*, "the two kites," as kites were birds of prey whose shrill cries resemble wailing.

Nephthys was always positioned protectively at the head of the coffin of the deceased, while Isis was at the feet, because that is how they had protected Osiris. Female and male mourners were divided into separate groups; the female group always appeared to be larger, consisting of not only female relatives but also professional mourners hired for the occasion. The women had their linen dresses tied below their breasts, so they were partially uncovered. Their long hair was loose and unkempt. They wailed and threw up their arms, threw dust over their heads, and wept. Scenes of this almost-choreographed anguish and lamenting have been referred to as a "performance of loss" (Riggs 2013: 158).

By the time of the New Kingdom, the main funeral ritual, "The Opening of the Mouth," was carried out on the mummy in the courtyard area in front of the tomb. This ritual's name comes from the fact that the mouth was the first of twenty-three parts of the deceased's body that was touched with specific objects so that the body could function again in the afterlife. The mouth was touched with an adze tipped with meteoritic iron so that the deceased could talk and eat again. After this funeral ritual was completed, the deceased was buried and, in the coming twelve hours of night, faced the judgment with the weighing of the heart and the passage to the afterlife. If one passed into the afterlife successfully, one became an *akh*, an "effective one," and lived again.

TOMB ARCHITECTURE AND DECORATION

Because funerary structures were to last for eternity, the ancient Egyptians built them, or cut them, out of stone. Although ancient Egyptian tombs differed in size and plan over time, they all fulfilled two specific functions. The substructure of the tomb under the ground protected the body, while the superstructure, above the ground, provided a place for a cult of the deceased. For the most part, nonroyal tombs of the Old Kingdom took the form of a "mastaba," which was built out of limestone blocks in a rectangular or bench shape. The name "mastaba" comes from the Arabic word for a bench. Good examples of mastabas can be seen at the Old Kingdom Fourth Dynasty (2613–2494 BCE) site of Giza.

The mastaba is basically solid except for a vertical shaft through the superstructure down to a small burial chamber, just large enough for the sarcophagus and some accompanying objects. After the burial, the entire shaft was filled with rubble and closed at the top with stone. The only space that opened up in the superstructure was a small L-shaped room in the southeast corner that functioned as a chapel for offerings for the deceased. The focal point of the chapel was a "false door" in the west wall. It is a stone replica of a door with an offering formula to feed the deceased along the top and then a depiction of the deceased sitting at a table of bread. Down along the sides are the titles and name of the deceased.

Often right behind the false door was a small hidden room called the "serdab," which is the Arabic word for a cellar. In the serdab was the *ka*-statue of the deceased, which the deceased could occupy. Sometimes servant statuettes were placed in the serdab as well, depicting, for example, a woman grinding grain and another woman mixing the mash for beer. The *ka* could also pass through the false door, and when the *ka*-priest arrived with food and drink for the deceased, the *ka* could partake of the sustenance and live. If the *ka*-priest could not come, the table of bread scene showed the deceased eating, and the carved offering formula with its hieroglyphic words for beer, bread, oxen, ducks, and other foods could feed the deceased. The servant statuettes could also feed the *ka*. Later in the Old Kingdom, more rooms were put into the mastaba, and the walls covered with scenes of daily life. There were scenes of life on the estate of the deceased with the growing of plants and rearing of animals. Then scenes closer to the false door showed male and female servants bringing food to the deceased.

A second type of tomb, the rock-cut tomb, was also used in the Old Kingdom, particularly in the provinces of Upper Egypt, where the tombs were cut into the limestone cliffs facing the Nile. Generally, a rock-cut tomb had a single chamber cut in the rock for the tomb chapel, and the burial chamber was a shaft cut down in the rock from the chamber floor. Both mastabas and rock-cut tombs continued to be used through the Middle Kingdom (2055–1650 BCE), but by the New Kingdom (1550–1295 BCE), a rock-cut tomb rather than a built tomb was the rule. The best examples of New Kingdom tombs can be seen on the West Bank of ancient Thebes where religious and government officials were buried. More than four hundred rock-cut tombs are known. The tombs can be large or small but follow a fairly typical plan.

An enclosed court was built with mudbrick walls in front of the rock face of the Theban mountain. In the rock at the back of the court, the entrance into the tomb chapel was cut. Sometimes a small brick pyramid was built over the doorway into the chapel. The shaft down to the burial chamber was cut out on the floor of the open court. The interior of the tomb chapel was arranged in a T shape, with a corridor going straight in from the door and a transverse corridor just inside the door. The interior walls were all painted with scenes. In the Eighteenth Dynasty, the walls were decorated with scenes of the official's daily life as well as the rituals for his burial, while in the later New Kingdom, religious scenes dominated.

In all these tombs, the focus is on the male person for whom it was built. As most women married, they were taken care of by their husbands and included into their tombs. The woman could have a *ka*-statue in her husband's serdab and also could be shown in the table of bread scene with him or could be shown with him in other scenes in the tomb. A wife was given a separate shaft down to a burial chamber, like her husband. Only rarely, however, did a woman, especially a nonroyal woman, have her own tomb. A tomb, like a mastaba at Giza, was granted to an official by the king, so a woman could not have a tomb like that, as women did not function as government officials. From what we know, if a woman was not buried with her husband, she could be buried with her father or added into a family tomb.

DOMESTIC CULTS FOR THE *AKH*, OR "SPIRIT," IN HOUSES AT DEIR EL-MEDINEH

In the second room of the houses in the workmen's village of Deir el-Medineh were niches in the wall that once held a stela or a bust of a family ancestor, who was thought of as having lived a good and moral life. In one house, excavators found three niches, and on the ground below were two ancestor busts that must have fallen out of them. This was a lucky find, as it provided unquestionable evidence for the use of the niches. These ancestors were referred to as an *akh iqer n Ra*, "an efficient spirit of Ra," meaning that this person had entered the afterlife and was in the company of gods such as Ra and Osiris. On these stone stelae, the ancestor is shown sitting in front of offerings and holding a lily, a symbol of rebirth. The stelae have inscriptions naming the ancestor and the person who set up the stelae and a short offering formula for them. A majority of the ancestors on the stelae are male. The busts are carved out of limestone, sandstone, or wood. They have no inscriptions and are often very worn or damaged, and their original paint is gone. This has made it very difficult for scholars to identify them as male or female, and it was possible that they were never meant to actually resemble a specific person. There are about ninety busts known from Deir el-Medineh, more than any other place in Egypt.

The stelae and the busts were the focus of a domestic cult that was concerned with solving personal and family problems in the household as well as continuing to remember the deceased. The ancestor was offered libations and food and was asked to act as an intermediary with a god or goddess to take care of a difficulty or problem. These ancestor stelae were also found in the chapels in the village, and so we can assume that they served the same purpose in both and could be worshipped in chapels and private houses and perhaps moved from one to the other.

LETTERS TO THE DEAD

Another way that the living made contact with relatives who had passed away takes the form of letters, referred to as "Letters to the Dead." There are only around two dozen of these letters known. The earliest are from the time of the later Old Kingdom, and they seem to stop by the end of the New Kingdom, a period lasting from about 2345 BCE to 1295 BCE. The early letters are written on clay vessels filled with a food offering, which were then placed at the tomb of the deceased. Later letters were written on papyri or sometimes a piece of limestone. The letters generally explain a problem that the living relative is having, such as illness, some kind of upset, or problem with inheritance, and either accuse the deceased of causing it or request that the deceased solve the problem. One of the most famous of these letters, dating from the New Kingdom, is from a man who writes to his deceased wife, describing their marriage and how kind and thoughtful he was always to her and how he has remained faithful to her for the three years since she died. He pleads, "What have I done against you wrongfully for you to get in this evil disposition in which you are?" (Wente 1990: 216). The letters to females seem in general to want to pacify them, reminding them of how much they are missed and that they must be kind to the household they left behind. It has been suggested that perhaps women addressed in some of these letters died in childbirth, and therefore having died prematurely may have been thought to be angry and malevolent sprits that had to be pacified (Schiavo 2020).

THE WISE WOMAN AT DEIR EL-MEDINEH

There are four short texts on ostraca (a pot sherd or piece of limestone used to write on) found at Deir el-Medineh that mention going to the wise woman or that someone should go to the wise woman. In ancient Egypt, this person was *ta rekhet*, "the knowing woman." One text, written by a man to a woman, asks her to go to the wise woman about his two boys who had died and find out if this was their fate. Another text is also about a death, and the person is told that it was caused by the manifestation of the god Ptah. Another person wants to know what manifestation of a deity has affected their eyes. The ancient Egyptians believed that gods and goddesses could punish them and cause illness, and the wise woman seems to have been the one to interpret what had happened and tell the person what to do, if anything. It also seems that the wise woman was consulted when children were sick. It is possible that a similar wise woman existed at other ancient Egyptian villages, but only at Deir el-Medineh, where a large amount of written evidence from the village was preserved, has the mention of her.

In 2014, the torso of a female mummy from a badly disturbed tomb at Deir el-Medineh was studied (Austin and Gobeil 2016). The head, legs, and hands were missing, but a large number of tattoos could be seen on the neck, torso, and arms. The neck was tattooed with *wadjet* eyes, sitting baboons, and *nefer* signs. The *wadjet* eyes are protective, baboons can be associated with Thoth who is a magician, and the meaning of the *nefer* sign is "good." Tattoos of snakes are in the three places: front of the shoulders, by the armpits, and on the right arm. Also on the right arm is a tattoo of a *sistrum* handle, and the left arm has small cows of Hathor and a papyrus plant. Lotus blossoms were tattooed on her lower back. Suggestions have been made that this woman could have been a wise woman, a magician, or a "scorpion charmer" who treats both scorpion and snake bites, or she could have functioned as all three. The tattoos that have Hathoric symbolism could fit into this explanation as well, as in later Ptolemaic times, Hathor is referred to as a wise woman. Perhaps Hathor was thought of in this way earlier as well.

AN ELITE THEBAN FESTIVAL BANQUET

Evidence for banquets in ancient Egypt is provided best in New Kingdom Theban tomb scenes from the Eighteenth Dynasty (1550–1295 BCE). These banquets most probably took place in the courtyard in front of the tomb and were tied to either the funeral celebration after the burial or a festival taking place in the necropolis of Thebes, on the West Bank, such as the "Beautiful Festival of the Valley," when the statue of the god Amun left his temple at Karnak, along with the statues of his wife, Mut, and his son, Khonsu, and crossed the river to visit each of the royal funerary temples. This was an annual festival that took place in the tenth month of the year. As the god visited the temples that took care of the cults of the deceased kings, the people from the city of Thebes had a holiday and visited the tombs of deceased members of their family.

A scene of a "Beautiful Festival of the Valley" banquet can be seen in the tomb of Userhat, Theban Tomb 56. Userhat served King Amenhotep II (1727–1400 BCE), and his most important title was "scribe who counts bread in Upper and Lower Egypt" (Hodel-Hoenes 2000: 65), which put him in charge of grain for the production of both flour and bread, the most important Egyptian food. His position included overseeing baking and supplying all the bread for the army rations, which explains why in other parts of the tomb army recruits are shown. His wife was named Mutnefert, "the goddess Mut is beautiful," and she carried the title of "royal ornament," reflecting a position of status within the king's court. Userhat and Mutnefert had two daughters. Their oldest daughter, Henutnefret, held the title "lady of the court, beloved of her Lord" (meaning "the king"), which possibly meant that she was raised at court with the king's daughters. Her father, Userhat, had been raised in the royal court and stated that in his autobiography in the tomb.

In the first offering scene of the banquet, Mutnefert sits next to her husband and holds on to his arm. She is wearing a full-length white linen gown with shoulder straps and a long wig, decorated with a lotus and topped with a cone of unguent. Under her chair are objects that belong to her: a mirror and a pet monkey who is tied to the back leg of the chair. Both the mirror and the monkey are things that are associated with the goddess Hathor, as is the drinking and music at the banquet. Mutnefert and her husband sit with offerings of food and drink in front of them. Their two daughters offer them a bowl of wine and a broad necklace, while their son, standing behind his sisters, holds up a "Bouquet of Amun" to them. This bouquet has in the center a large open water lily, which symbolizes birth, or in this case in a tomb scene, rebirth in the afterlife.

In a register below this scene, the guests at the banquet are shown smaller in size. The guests are sitting, with women and men divided into two groups. It is not known if this is realistic and that in an actual ancient banquet, women and men were separated. The women are sitting on thick mats, with unguent cones on their heads.

Their hands reach for bowls of wine, given by a female servant. In one hand, the servant holds a very small vessel that is thought to contain some kind of narcotic to enhance the effect of the wine. The scene with the male guests is quite damaged. They are sitting on stools or chairs that are quite high, under a grapevine. They also have flower collars and unguent cones, but the detail is hard to see.

Another of these scenes depicts musicians and singers. There is a male harpist sitting and playing, and behind him sit three females; the first plays a double flute, while the next two clap their hands, so perhaps they were singers. There are further figures behind them, but they are damaged. A banquet like this would take place in the courtyard right outside the tomb, and probably the festivities would go on all night. At such a festival, it was expected for both women and men to become very inebriated, to the point of ecstasy, or having an epiphany. Drinking too much seems to have been looked down on in daily Egyptian life, but in the context of a religious festival, it was accepted and, in fact, expected.

DOCUMENT: HEMIRA, PRIESTESS OF THE GODDESS HATHOR, FALSE DOOR

This is a translation of the right half of the false door of a woman named Hemira who was a priestess of the goddess Hathor. In fact, that was her only title. The limestone false door was found at the site of Busiris and dates to the very late Old Kingdom around 2160 BCE. It is the only known monument with her name; her actual tomb has never been found. Hemira mentions her husband in the text but not by name, and she is the only person depicted on the false door. When the text talks about her "good name," that is a way ancient Egyptians referred to a nickname.

The long offering text on the right jamb of the door reads:

An offering which the king gives and which Anubis, foremost of the divine booth who is in his wrappings, lord of the sacred land, gives, may offerings be given in the *wag*-festival and the festival of Thoth, for the justified Hemira, her good name is Hemi.

The shorter text on the inner jamb next to it reads:

"I gave bread to the hungry and clothes to the naked, praised of her husband, Hemira. As for anyone who will say bread and beer for Hemi in this her tomb, I am an excellent spirit, I will not do evil to them."

Source: The drawing of the false door in Fischer, Henry. *Egyptian Women of the Old Kingdom and of the Heracleopolitan Period*. New York, 2000, p. 40, fig. 30. Text translated by Lisa Sabbahy.

BIBLIOGRAPHY

Allen, James. 2005. *The Art of Medicine in Ancient Egypt*. New York: Metropolitan Museum of Art.

Andrews, Carol. 1990. *Ancient Egyptian Jewellery*. London: British Museum Press.

Andrews, Carol. 1994. *Amulets of Ancient Egypt*. London: British Museum Press.

Arnold, Dieter. 2009. *The Monuments of Egypt: An A–Z Companion to Ancient Egyptian Architecture*. Cairo: American University in Cairo Press.

Arnold, Dorothea. 1996. *The Royal Women of Amarna*. New York: Metropolitan Museum of Art.

Arnold, Dorothea. 1999. *When the Pyramids Were Built: Egyptian Art of the Old Kingdom*. New York: Metropolitan Museum of Art.

Assmann, Jan. 2001. *Death and Salvation in Ancient Egypt*. Ithaca, NY and London: Cornell University Press.

Baines, John, and Jaromír Málek. 1980. *Atlas of Ancient Egypt*. Oxford: Facts on File.

Bierbrier, Morris. 1989. *The Tomb-Builders of the Pharaohs*. Cairo: American University in Cairo Press.

Brewer, Douglas. 2005. *Ancient Egypt: Foundations of a Civilization*. Harlow, England: Pearson Education Limited.

Capel, Anne, and Glenn Markoe. 1996. *Mistress of the House, Mistress of Heaven: Women in Ancient Egypt*. New York: Hudson Hills Press.

Collier, Mark, and Bill Manley. 1998. *How to Read Egyptian Hieroglyphs*. Berkeley and Los Angeles: University of California Press.

David, Rosalie (ed.). 2008. *Egyptian Mummies and Modern Science*. Cambridge: Cambridge University Press.

David, Rosalie, and Rick Archbold. 2000. *Conversations with Mummies*. New York: Madison Press.

Dawson, Julie, and Helen Strudwick. 2016. *Death in the Nile: Uncovering the Afterlife of Ancient Egypt*. London: Fitzwilliam Museum.

Dodson, Aidan. 2009. *Amarna Sunset, Nefertiti. Tutankhamun, Ay, Horemheb, and the Egyptian Counter-Reformation*. Cairo: American University in Cairo Press.

Dodson, Aidan. 2014. *Amarna Sunrise, Egypt from Golden Age to Age of Heresy*. Cairo: American University in Cairo Press.

Dodson, Aidan. 2019. *Rameses III, King of Egypt*. Cairo: American University in Cairo Press.

Donker van Heel, Koenraad. 2016. *Mrs. Naunakhte & Family: The Women of Ramesside Deir al-Medina*. Cairo: American University in Cairo Press.

Eaton-Krauss, Marianne. 2016. *The Unknown Tutankhamun*. London: Bloomsbury.

Fagan, Brian. 1975. *The Rape of the Nile: Tomb Robbers, Tourist, and Archaeologists in Egypt*. New York: Charles Scriber's Sons.

Freed, Rita, Lawrence Berman, Denise Doxey, and Nicholas Picardo. 2009. *The Secrets of Tomb 10A: Egypt 2000 BC*. Boston: Museum of Fine Arts.

Galán, José, Betsy Bryan, and Peter Dorman (eds.). 2014. *Creativity and Innovation in the Reign of Hatshepsut*. Chicago: Oriental Institute of the University of Chicago.

Gardiner, Alan. 1988. *Egyptian Grammar*. Cambridge: Cambridge University Press.

Graves-Brown, Carolyn (ed.). 2008. *Sex and Gender in Ancient Egypt: "Don Your Wig for a Joyful Hour."* Swansea: Classical Press of Wales.

Graves-Brown, Carolyn. 2010. *Dancing for Hathor: Women in Ancient Egypt*. London: Continuum.

Habachi, Labib. 1977. *The Obelisks of Egypt: Skyscrapers of the Past*. New York: Charles Scribner's Sons.

Hawass, Zahi, and Sahar Saleem. 2019. *Scanning the Pharaohs: CT Imaging of the New Kingdom Royal Mummies*. Cairo: American University in Cairo Press.

Hayes, William. 1953. *The Scepter of Egypt: A Background for the Study of the Egyptian Antiquities in the Metropolitan Museum of Art*. New York: Metropolitan Museum of Art.

Hornung, Erik. 1992. *Idea into Image: Essays on Ancient Egyptian Thought*. New York: Timken Publishers.

Hornung, Erik. 1999. *The Ancient Egyptian Books of the Afterlife*. Ithaca, NY and London: Cornell University Press.

Imhausen, Annette. 2016. *Mathematics in Ancient Egypt, A Contextual History*. Princeton, NJ, and Oxford: Princeton University Press.

James, Thomas. 2003. *Pharaoh's People: Scenes from Life in Imperial Egypt*. London: I.B. Taurus.

Kemp, Barry. 2006. *Ancient Egypt: Anatomy of a Civilization*. London and New York: Routledge.

Kemp, Barry. 2012. *The City of Akhenaten and Nefertiti, Amarna and Its People*. Cairo: American University in Cairo Press.

Kemp, Barry. 2005. *100 Hieroglyphs: Think Like an Egyptian*. London: Granta Books.

Kitchen, Kenneth. 1982. *Pharaoh Triumphant: The Life and Times of Ramesses II*. Warminster, England: Aris and Phillips.

Lehner, Mark, and Zahi Hawass. 2017. *Giza and the Pyramids*. Cairo: American University in Cairo Press.

Malek, Jaromir. 1986. *In the Shadow of the Pyramids, Egypt during the Old Kingdom*. Cairo: American University in Cairo Press.

Malek, Jaromir. 1993. *The Cat in Ancient Egypt*. London: British Museum Press.

Manniche, Lise. 1989. *An Ancient Egyptian Herbal*. Austin: University of Texas Press.

McDowell, Andrea G. 1999. *Village Life in Ancient Egypt: Laundry Lists and Love Songs*. Oxford: Oxford University Press.

Meskell, Lynn. 2002. *Private Life in New Kingdom Egypt*. Princeton, NJ, and Oxford: Princeton University Press.

Moeller, Nadine. 2016. *The Archaeology of Urbanism in Ancient Egypt: From the Predynastic Period to the End of the Middle Kingdom*. New York: Cambridge University Press.

O'Conner, David, and Eric Cline. 2001. *Amenhotep III: Perspectives on His Reign*. Ann Arbor: University of Michigan Press.

Oppenheim, Adela, Dorothea Arnold, Dieter Arnold, and Kei Yamamoto (eds.). 2015. *Ancient Egypt Transformed: The Middle Kingdom*. New York: Metropolitan Museum of Art.

Parkinson, Richard, and Stephen Quirke. 1995. *Papyrus*. Austin: University of Texas Press.

Patch, Diana. 2011. *Dawn of Egyptian Art*. New York. Metropolitan Museum of Art.

Pinch, Geraldine. 1994. *Magic in Ancient Egypt*. London. British Museum Press.

Pinch, Geraldine. 2004. *Egyptian Myth: A Very Short Introduction*. Oxford: Oxford University Press.

Quirke, Stephen. 1992. *Ancient Egyptian Religion*. London: British Museum Press.

Quirke, Stephen, and Jeffry Spencer. 1992. *The British Museum Book of Ancient Egypt*. London: British Museum.

Raven, Maarten. 2010. *Egyptian Magic: The Quest for Thoth's Book of Secrets*. Cairo: American University on Cairo Press.

Redford, Donald. 1984. *Akhenaten: The Heretic King*. Princeton, NJ: Princeton University Press.

Reeves, Nicholas. 1990. *The Complete Tutankhamun*. Cairo: American University in Cairo Press.

Reeves, Nicolas. 2000. *Ancient Egypt: The Great Discoveries*. New York: Thames and Hudson.

Robins, Gay. 1993. *Women in Ancient Egypt*. London: British Museum Press.

Robins, Gay. 1997. *The Art of Ancient Egypt*. London: British Museum Press.

Roehrig, Catherine (ed.). 2006. *Hatshepsut from Queen to Pharaoh*. New York: Metropolitan Museum of Art.

Ruffle, John. 1977. *The Egyptians*. Ithaca, NY: Cornell University Press.

Scalf, Foy (ed.). 2017. *Book of the Dead, Becoming God in Ancient Egypt*. Chicago: Oriental Institute of the University of Chicago.

Schulz, Regine, and Matthias Seidel. 2009. *Egyptian Art: The Walters Art Museum*. London: Giles.

Seyfried, Friederike. 2012. *In the Light of Amarna: 100 Years of the Nefertiti Discovery*. Petersberg, Germany: Michael Imhof Verlag.

Shafer, Byron (ed.). 1991. *Religion in Ancient Egypt: Gods, Myths and Personal Practice*. Ithaca, NY, and London: Cornell University Press.

Shaw, Garry. 2012. *The Pharaoh: Life at Court and on Campaign*. London: Thames and Hudson.

Shaw, Ian (ed.). 2000. *The Oxford History of Ancient Egypt*. Oxford: Oxford University Press.

Shaw, Ian. 2012. *Ancient Egyptian Technology and Innovation*. London: Bristol Classical Press.

Shaw, Ian, and Paul Nicholson. 2008. *The Illustrated Dictionary of Ancient Egypt*. Cairo: American University in Cairo Press.

Smith, Mark. 2017. *Following Osiris: Perspectives on the Osirian Afterlife from Four Millennia*. Oxford: Oxford University Press.

Snape, Steven. 2014. *The Complete Cities of Ancient Egypt*. London: Thames and Hudson.

Spencer, Alan Jeffrey. 1988. *Death in Ancient Egypt*. London: Penguin Books.

Stevenson, Alice (ed.). 2015. *The Petrie Museum of Egyptian Archaeology*. London: UCL Press.

Szpakowska, Kasia (ed.). 2006. *Through a Glass Darkly: Magic, Dreams and Prophecy in Ancient Egypt*. Swansea: Classical Press of Wales.

Taylor, John. 2004. *Mummy: The Inside Story*. London: British Museum Press.

Taylor, John. 2010a. *Egyptian Mummies*. London: British Museum Press.

Taylor, John. 2010b. *Spells for Eternity: The Ancient Egyptian Book of the Dead*. London: British Museum Press.

Taylor, John, and Daniel Antoine. 2014. *Ancient Lives: New Discoveries: Eight Mummies, Eight Stories*. London: British Museum Press.

Teeter, Emily (ed.). 2011a. *Before the Pyramids: The Origins of Egyptian Civilization*. Chicago: Oriental Institute of the University of Chicago.

Teeter, Emily. 2011b. *Religion and Ritual in Ancient Egypt*. Cambridge. Cambridge University Press.

Teeter, Emily, and Janet Johnson (eds.). 2009. *The Life of Meresamun: A Temple Singer in Ancient Egypt*. Chicago: Oriental Institute of the University of Chicago.

Thomas, Nancy. 1995. *The American Discovery of Ancient Egypt*. Los Angeles: Los Angeles County Museum of Art.

Tyldesley, Joyce. 2006. *The Complete Queens of Egypt*. Cairo: American University in Cairo Press.

Wendrich, Willeke. 2010. *Egyptian Archaeology*. Chichester, England: Wiley-Blackwell.

Wilkinson, Alix. 1998. *The Garden in Ancient Egypt*. London: Rubicon Press.

Wilkinson, Richard. 1992. *Reading Egyptian Art: A Hieroglyphic Guide to Ancient Egyptian Painting and Sculpture*. London: Thames and Hudson.

Wilkinson, Richard. 2008. *Egyptian Scarabs*. Oxford: Shire Egyptology.

Wilkinson, Toby. 1999. *Early Dynastic Egypt*. London and New York: Routledge.

Wilkinson, Toby. 2007. *Lives of the Ancient Egyptians*. London: Thames and Hudson.

Winlock, Herbert. 2010. *Tutankhamun's Funeral*. New York: Metropolitan Museum of Art.

Ziegler, Christiane. 2008. *Queens of Egypt: From Hetepheres to Cleopatra*. Monaco: Grimaldi Forum.

SOCIETY AND FAMILY LIFE

Černy, Jaroslav. 1945. "The Will of Naunakhte and the Related Documents." *Journal of Egyptian Archaeology* 31, 29–53.

Edwards, Iorwerth Eiddon. 1960. *Hieratic Papyri in the British Museum*. London: British Museum Press.

Eyre, Christopher. 1992. "The Adoption Papyrus in Social Context." *Journal of Egyptian Archaeology* 78, 207–22.

Janssen, Rosalind, and Jac Janssen. 1990. *Growing Up in Ancient Egypt*. London: Rubicon Press.

Kemp, Barry. 2006. *Ancient Egypt: Anatomy of a Civilization*. London and New York: Routledge.

Lichtheim, Miriam. 1973. *Ancient Egyptian Literature*. Vol. 1. Berkeley: University of California Press.

Lichtheim, Miriam. 1976. *Ancient Egyptian Literature*. Vol. 2. Berkeley: University of California Press.

McDowell, Andrea. 1999. *Village Life in Ancient Egypt: Laundry Lists and Love Songs*. Oxford: Oxford University Press.

Oldfather, Charles H., trans. 1989. *Diodorus of Sicily*. Cambridge, MA: Harvard University Press.

Parkinson, Richard. 1991. *Voices from Ancient Egypt: An Anthology of Middle Kingdom Writing*. London: British Museum Press.

Picardo, Nicholas. 2006. "Egypt's Well-to-Do, Elite Mansions in the Town of Wah-Sut." *Expedition* 48, 37–40.

Riddle, John. *Contraception and Abortion from the Ancient World to the Renaissance*. Cambridge, MA: Harvard University Press.

Robins, Gay. 1993. *Women in Ancient Egypt*. London: British Museum Press.

Strouhal, Eugen. 2008. *The Memphite Tomb of Horemheb Commander-in-Chief of Tutankhamun: IV Human Skeletal Remains*. London: Egypt Exploration Society.

Strudwick, Nigel. 2005. *Texts from the Pyramid Age*. Atlanta: Society of Biblical Literature.

Sweeney, Deborah. 2004. "Forever Young? The Representation of Older and Ageing Women in Ancient Egyptian Art." *Journal of the American Research Center in Egypt* 41, 67–84.

Toivari-Viitala, Jana. 2001. *Women at Deir el-Medina*. Leiden, the Netherlands: Nederlands Instituut Voor Het Nabije Oosten.

Wegner, Josef. 2009. "A Decorated Birth-Brick from South Abydos: New Evidence on Childbirth and Birth Magic in the Middle Kingdom." In *Archaism and Innovation: Studies in the Culture of Middle Kingdom Egypt*, edited by David Silverman, William Kelly Simpson, and Josef Wegner, 447–96. New Haven, CT, and Philadelphia: Yale University and University of Pennsylvania Museum.

Whale, Sheila. 1989. *The Family in the Eighteenth Dynasty of Egypt*. Sydney: Australian Centre for Egyptology.

WORK, ECONOMY, AND LAW

Buck, Adrian de. 1937. "The Judicial Papyrus of Turin." *Journal of Egyptian Archaeology* 23, 152–64.

Dodson, Aidan. 2019. *Rameses III, King of Egypt: His Life and Afterlife*. Cairo: American University in Cairo Press.

Donker van Heel, Koenraad. 2016. *Mrs. Naunakhte & Family: The Women of Ramesside Deir al-Medina*. Cairo: American University in Cairo Press.

Fischer, Henry. 1976. *Varia. Egyptian Studies I*. New York: Metropolitan Museum of Art.

Fischer, Henry. 2000. *Egyptian Women of the Old Kingdom and of the Heracleopolitan Period*. New York: Metropolitan Museum of Art.

Graves-Brown, Carolyn. 2010. *Dancing for Hathor: Women in Ancient Egypt*. London: Continuum.

Hudáková, Lubica. 2019. *The Representations of Women in the Middle Kingdom Tombs of Officials*. Leiden, the Netherlands and Boston: Brill.

Lichtheim, Miriam. 1976. *Ancient Egyptian Literature: A Book of Readings.* Vol. 2. Berkeley: University of California Press.

Roehrig, Catharine. 1996. "Women's Work: Some Occupations of Non-royal Women as Depicted in Ancient Egyptian Art." In *Mistress of the House, Mistress of Heaven: Women in Ancient Egypt,* edited by Anne Capel and Glenn Markoe, 13–24. New York: Hudson Hill Press.

Routledge, Carolyn. 2008. "Did Women 'Do Things' in Ancient Egypt?" In *Sex and Gender in Ancient Egypt: "Don Your Wig for a Joyful Hour,"* edited by Carolyn Graves-Brown, 157–77. Swansea: Classical Press of Wales.

Sweeney, Deborah. 2006. "Women Growing Older in Deir el-Medina." In *Living and Writing in Deir el-Medine,* edited by Andreas Dorn and Tobias Hofmann, 135–59. Basel: Schwabe.

Wente, Edward. 1990. *Letters from Ancient Egypt.* Atlanta: Scholars Press.

Zivie, Alain. 2007. *The Lost Tombs of Saqqara.* Toulouse: Publicado por Caracara.

LITERACY, EDUCATION, AND HEALTH

Abdelfattah, Alia, Adel Alam, Samuel Wann, Randall Thompson, Goma Abdel-Maksoud, Ibrahem Badr, Hany Amer, Abd el-Halim Nur el-Din, Caleb Finch, and Michael Miyamoto. 2013. "Atherosclerotic Cardiovascular Disease in Egyptian Women: 1570 BCE–2011 CE." *International Journal of Cardiology* 167, no. 2, 570–74.

Allon, Niv, and Hana Navratilova. 2018. *Ancient Egyptian Scribes: A Cultural Exploration.* London: Bloomsbury Academic.

Bryan, Betsy. 1985. "Evidence for Female Literacy from Theban Tombs of the New Kingdom." *Bulletin of the Egyptological Seminar* 6, 17–32.

Cline, Eric, and David O'Connor. 2006. *Thutmose III: A New Biography.* Ann Arbor, MI: University of Michigan Press.

Dabbs, Gretchen, and Jerome Rose. 2016. "Report on the October 2015 Skeletal Analysis of the North Tombs Cemetery Project." *Journal of Egyptian Archaeology* 102, 7–10.

Donoghue, Helen, Oona Lee, David Minnikin, Gurdyal Besra, John Taylor, and Mark Spigelman. 2010. "Tuberculosis in Dr. Granville's Mummy: A Molecular Re-Examination of the Earliest Known Egyptian Mummy to Be Scientifically Examined and Given a Medical Diagnosis." *Proceedings of the Royal Society, Biology* 277, 51–56.

Fischer, Henry G. 1976. *Varia, Egyptian Studies 1.* New York: Metropolitan Museum of Art.

Forshaw, Robert. 2010. "Were the Dentists in Ancient Egypt Operative Dental Surgeons or Were They Pharmacists?" In *Pharmacy and Medicine in Ancient Egypt: Proceedings of the Conferences Held in Cairo (2007) and Manchester (2008),* edited by Jenefer Cockitt and Rosalie David, 72–77. Oxford: BAR International Series, 2141.

Hassan, Selim. 1932. *Excavations at Giza, 1929–1930*. Oxford: Oxford University Press.

Lichtheim, Miriam. 1976. *Ancient Egyptian Literature: A Book of Readings*. Berkeley: University of California Press.

Majno, Guido. 1975. *The Healing Hand: Man and Wound in the Ancient World*. Cambridge, MA: Harvard University Press.

Riddle, John. 1992. *Contraception and Abortion from the Ancient World to the Renaissance*. Cambridge, MA: Harvard University Press.

Robins, Gay. 1993. *Women in Ancient Egypt*. London: British Museum Press.

Roehrig, Catharine. 2005. "Senenmut, Royal Tutor to Princess Neferure." In *Hatshepsut from Queen to Pharaoh*, edited by Catharine Roehrig, 112–16. New York: Metropolitan Museum of Art.

Schulz, Regine, and Matthias Seidel. 2009. *Egyptian Art: The Walters Art Museum*. London: Giles.

Smith-Guzmán, Nicole. 2015. "The Skeletal Manifestation of Malaria: An Epidemiological Approach Using Documented Skeletal Collections." *American Journal of Physical Anthropology* 158, 631.

Strouhal, Eugen, Bretislav Vachala, and Hana Vymazalová. 2014. *The Medicine of the Ancient Egyptians*. Vol. 1, *Surgery, Gynecology, Obstetrics, Pediatrics*. Cairo: American University in Cairo Press.

Teeter, Emily. 2009. "Meresamun's Egypt." In *The Life of Meresamun: A Temple Singer in Ancient Egypt*, edited by Emily Teeter and Janet Johnson, 15–24. Chicago: Oriental Institute Museum Publications.

Thompson, Randall, Adel Allam, Albert Zink, Samuel Wann, Guido Lombardi, Samantha Cox, Bruno Frohlich, Linda Sutherland, James Sutherland, and Thomas Frohlich. 2014. "Computed Tomographic Evidence of Atherosclerosis in the Mummified Remains of Humans from Around the World." *Global Heart* 9, no. 2, 187–96.

Vannier, Michael. 2009. "CT Scanning of Meresamun." In *The Life of Meresamun: A Temple Singer in Ancient Egypt*, edited by Emily Teeter and Janet Johnson, 111–18. Chicago: Oriental Institute Museum Publications.

Zink, Albert, Waltraud Grabner, Udo Reischl, Hans Wolf, and Andreas Nerlich. 2003. "Molecular Study on Human Tuberculosis in Three Geographically Distinct and Time Delineated Populations from Ancient Egypt." *Epidmiology and Infection* 130, no. 2, 239–49.

PERSONAL PROPERTY

Davies, Norman de Garis. 1929. "The Town House in Ancient Egypt." *Metropolitan Museum Studies* 1, no. 2, 233–55.

Fletcher, Joann. 1998. "The Secrets of the Locks Unraveled." *Nekhen News* 10, 7–9.

Janssen, Rosalind, and Jac Janssen. 1989. *Egyptian Household Animals*. Aylesbury: Shire Egyptology.

Kanawati, Naguib, and Mohamed Abder-Raziq. 2008. *Mereruka and His Family, Part II, The Tomb of Waatetkhethor*. Oxford: Australian Centre for Egyptology.

Kemp, Barry. 1987. "The Amarna Workmen's Village in Retrospect." *Journal of Egyptian Archaeology* 73, 21–50.

Killen, Geoffrey. 1994. *Egyptian Woodworking and Furniture*. Buckinghamshire: Shire Egyptology.

Koltsida, Aikaterini. 2007. *Social Aspects of Ancient Egyptian Domestic Architecture*. Oxford: British Archaeological Reports.

Lang, Elizabeth. 2016. "Maids at the Grindstone: A Comparative Study of New Kingdom Grain Grinders." *Journal of Lithic Studies* 3, no. 3, 279–89.

Manniche, Lise. 1999. *Egyptian Luxuries: Fragrance, Aromatherapy, and Cosmetics in Pharaonic Times*. Cairo: American University in Cairo Press.

Nelson-Hurst, Melinda. 2017. "Spheres of Economic and Administrative Control in Middle Kingdom Egypt: Textual, Visual, and Archaeological Evidence for Female and Male Sealers." In *Structures of Power, Law and Gender across the Ancient Near East and Beyond*, edited by Ilan Peled, 131–42. Chicago: Oriental Institute of the University of Chicago.

Picardo, Nicholas. 2015. "Hybrid Households: Institutional Affiliations and Household Identity in the Town of Wah-Sut (South Abydos)." In *Household Studies in Complex Societies: (Micro) Archaeological and Textual Approaches*, edited by Miriam Müller, 243–88. Chicago: Oriental Institute Seminars.

Quirke, Stephen. 2005. *Lahun: A Town in Egypt 1800 BC, and the History of Its Landscape*. London: Golden House Publications.

Reisner, George. 1955. *A History of the Giza Necropolis*. Vol. 2, *The Tomb of Hetep-Heres the Mother of Cheops*. Cambridge, MA: Harvard University Press.

Spence, Kate. 2004. "The Three-Dimensional Form of the Amarna House." *Journal of Egyptian Archaeology* 90, 123–52.

Spence, Kate. 2015. "Ancient Egyptian Houses and Households: Architecture, Artifacts, Conceptualization, and Interpretation." In *Household Studies in Complex Societies: (Micro) Archaeological and Textual Approaches*, edited by Miriam Müller, 83–100. Chicago: Oriental Institute Seminars.

Stead, Mariam. 1986. *Egyptian Life*. London: British Museum.

Szpakowska, Kasia. 2008. *Daily Life in Ancient Egypt*. Malden, MA; Oxford:Wiley.

Vassilika, Eleni. 2010. *The Tomb of Kha*. Florence: Fondazione Museo delle Antichità Egizie di Torino

Vogelsang-Eastwood, Gillian. 1993. *Pharaonic Egyptian Clothing*. Leiden, the Netherlands; New York; Köln, Germany: Brill.

Wilson, Hilary.1988. *Egyptian Food and Drink*. Aylesbury, England: Shire Egyptology.

ENTERTAINMENT

Bryan, Betsy. 2014. "Hatshepsut and Cultic Revelries in the New Kingdom." In *Creativity and Innovation in the Reign of Hatshepsut*, edited
by José Galán, Betsy Bryan and Peter Dorman, 93–124. Chicago: The
Oriental Institute of the University of Chicago.

David, Rosalie. 1979. "Toys and Games from Kahun in the Manchester
Museum Collection." In *Glimpses of Ancient Egypt, Studies in Hon-
our of H.W. Fairman*, edited by John Ruffle, G. Gaballa, and Kenneth
Kitchen, 12–15. Warminster, England: Aris and Phillips.

Foster, John. 1974. *Love Songs of the New Kingdom*. New York: Charles
Scribner.

Harrington, Nicola. 2016. "The Eighteenth Dynasty Egyptian Banquet: Ideals and Realities." In *Dining and Death: Interdisciplinary Perspectives
on the "Funerary Banquet" in Ancient Art, Burial and Belief* (Paper 4,
50 pages), edited by Catherine Draycott and Maria Stamatopoulou,
129–71. Leuven, Belgium: Peeters.

Kanawati, Naguib, and Mahmoud Abder-Raziq. 2008. *Mereruka and His Family, Part II, The Tomb of Waatetkhethor*. Oxford: Aris and Phillips Ltd.

Lichtheim, Mariam. 1973. Literature of Ancient Egypt, vol. 1. Berkeley:
University of California Press.

Manniche, Lise. 1991. *Music and Musicians in Ancient Egypt*. London: British Museum Press.

Morris, Ellen. 2011. "Paddle Dolls and Performance." *Journal of the American Research Center in Egypt* 47, 71–103.

Roehrig, Catherine. 2015. "Two Tattooed Women from Thebes." *Bulletin of
the Egyptological Seminar* 19, 527–36.

Szpakowska, Kasia. 2003. "Altered States: An Inquiry into the Possible
Use of Narcotics or Alcohol to Induce Dreams in Pharaonic Egypt."
In *A Delta-man in Yebu, Occasional Volume of the Egyptologists' Elec-
tronic Forum, No. 1*, edited by A. K. Eyma and C. J. Bennett. Irvine,
California: Universal Publishers.

Teeter, Emily. 1993. "Female Musicians in Pharaonic Egypt." In *Redis-
covering the Muses: Women's Musical Traditions*, edited by Kimberly
Marshall, 68–91. Boston: Northeastern University Press.

Teeter, Emily, and Janet Johnson. 2009. *The Life of Meresamun: A Temple
Singer in Ancient Egypt*. Chicago: The Oriental Institute of the University of Chicago.

Touny, Ahmad D., and Steffen Wenig. 1969. *Sport in Ancient Egypt*. Leipzig,
Germany: Edition Leipzig.

Tyldesley, Joyce. 2007. *Egyptian Games and Sports*. Buckinghamshire: Shire
Egyptology.

THE LIFE OF ROYAL WOMEN

Allen, James. 2005. *The Ancient Egyptian Pyramid Texts*. Atlanta: Society of
Biblica Literature.

Bestock, Laurel. 2011. "The First Kings of Egypt: The Abydos Evidence." In *Before the Pyramids: The Origins of Egyptian Civilization,* edited by Emily Teeter, 137–44. Chicago: University of Chicago Press.

Kitchen, Kenneth. 1982. *Pharaoh Triumphant: The Life and Times of Ramesses II.* Warminster, England: Aris and Phillps.

Labrousse, Audran. 2012. "Recent Discoveries at the Necropolis of King Pepy I." In *Ancient Memphis, 'Enduring is the Perfection,'* edited by Linda Evans, 299–308. Leuven, Belgium and Paris: Peeters.

Picton, Jan. 2016. "Living and Working in a New Kingdom 'Harem Town.'" In *Women in Antiquity: Real Women across the Ancient World,* edited by Stephanie Budin and Jean Turfa, 229–42. London and New York: Routledge.

Redford, Donald. 1967. *History and Chronology of the Eighteenth Dynasty of Egypt: Seven Studies.* Toronto: University of Toronto Press.

Redford, Donald. 1984. *Akhenaten: The Heretic King.* Princeton: University of Princeton Press.

Robins, Gay. 1993. *Women in Ancient Egypt.* London: British Museum Press.

Roehrig, Catherine. 1999. "172. Pair Statue of Queen Ankh-nes-meryre II and Her Son Pepi II Seated." In *Egyptian Art in the Age of the Pyramids,* 437–39. New York: Metropolitan Museum of Art.

Sabbahy, Lisa. 1998. "The King's Mother in the Old Kingdom with Special Reference to the Title st-ntr." *Studien zur Altägyptischen Kultur* 25, 305–10.

Troy, Lana. 1986. *Patterns of Queenship in Ancient Myth and History.* Uppsala, Sweden: Almqvist and Wiksell.

Ziegler, Christine. 2008. *Queens of Egypt: From Hetepheres to Cleopatra.* Monaco: Grimaldi Forum.

RELIGIOUS LIFE AND THE AFTERLIFE

Assmann, Jan. 2001. *Death and Salvation in Ancient Egypt.* Ithaca, NY: Cornell University Press.

Austin, Anne, and Cedric Gobeil. 2016. "Embodying the Divine: A Tattooed Female Mummy from Deir el-Medina." *Bulletin de L'Institut Français D'Archéologie Orientale* 116, 23–46.

Demaree, Robert. 1983. *The 3h ikr n R'-Stelae: On Ancestor Worship in Ancient Egypt.* Leiden, the Netherlands: Nederlands Instituut voor het Nabije Oosten.

Faulkner, Raymond. 1972. *The Ancient Egyptian Book of the Dead.* London: British Museum Press.

Harrington, Nicole. 2016. "The Eighteenth Dynasty Banquets: Ideals and Realities." In *Dining and Death: Interdisciplinary Perspectives on the "Funerary Banquet" in Ancient Art, Burial and Belief,* edited by Catherine Draycott and Maria Stamatopoulou, 129–71. Leuven, Belgium: Peeters.

Hodel-Hoenes, Sigrid. 2000. *Life and Death in Ancient Egypt: Scenes from Private Tombs in New Kingdom Thebes*. Ithaca, NY: Cornell University Press.

Keith, Jean L. 2011. *Anthropoid Busts of Deir el Medineh and Other Sites and Collections*. Cairo: Institut Français d'Archéologie Orientale.

Kemp, Barry. 1995. "How Religious Were the Ancient Egyptians?" *Cambridge Archaeological Journal* 5, no. 1, 25–54.

Marochetti, Elise, Cinzia Oliva, Kristine Doneux, Alessandra Curti, and Francis Janot. 2005. "The Mummies of Kha and Merit: Embalming Ritual and Restoration Work." *Journal of Biological Research* 80, 243–47.

Riggs, Christina. 2013. "Mourning Women and Decorum in Ancient Egyptian Art." In *Decorum and Experience: Essays in Ancient Culture for John Baines*, edited by Elizabeth Frood and Angela McDonald, 156–62. Oxford: Griffith Institute Publications.

Schiavo, Renata. 2020. "Ghosts and Ancestors in a Gender Perspective." *Journal of Egyptian Interconnections* 25, 201–12.

Stevens, Chris, and Alan Clapham. 2014. "Botanical Insights into the Life of an Ancient Egyptian Village: Excavation Results from Amarna." In *Archaeology of African Plant Use*, edited by Chris Stevens, Sam Nixon, Mary Murray, and Dorian Fuller, 151–64. Walnut Creek, CA: Left Coast Press.

Sweeney, Deborah. 2014. "Sitting Happily with Amun." In *The Workman's Progress: Studies in the Village of Deir el-Medina and Other Documents from Western Thebes in Honour of Rob Demarée*, edited by B. J. Haring, O. E. Kaper, and R. van Walsem, 217–31. Leuven, Belgium: Peeters.

Vassilika, Eleni. 2010. *The Tomb of Kha*. Turin, Italy: Fondazione Museo delle Antichita Egizie.

Weatherhead, Fran, and Barry Kemp. 2007. *The Main Chapel at the Amarna Workmen's Village and Its Wall Paintings*. London: Egypt Exploration Society.

Wente, Edward. 1990. *Letters from Ancient Egypt*. Atlanta: Scholars Press.

INDEX

About the Author

LISA K. SABBAHY holds a PhD from the University of Toronto in Egyptian Archaeology. She is an assistant professor of Egyptology at the American University in Cairo (AUC), where she also serves as the director of the MA program in Egyptology and Coptology. Sabbahy's particular areas of special interest are royal women and their titles, the position and status of ancient Egyptian women, infectious diseases in ancient Egypt, and the iconography and role of the ancient Egyptian god, Nefertem.

Her most recent publications include *All Things Ancient Egypt: An Encyclopedia of the Ancient Egyptian World* (Greenwood, 2019); "King's Mother in the Old and Middle Kingdoms," *Routledge Companion to Women and Monarchy in the Ancient Mediterranean World* (2020); "Did Akhenaten's Founding of Akhetaten Cause a Malaria Epidemic?" *Journal of the American Research Center in Egypt* (2020); and *Kingship, Power, and Legitimacy in Ancient Egypt: From the Old Kingdom to the Middle Kingdom* (Cambridge University Press, 2020).

At AUC, Sabbahy teaches a wide variety of Egyptology courses but has most regularly taught History of Ancient Egypt, Archaeological and Historical Method and Theory, Material Culture, Gender in Ancient Egypt, and Research Design and Writing.